I DON'T MAKE THEM UP!

Reflections, Stories and Jokes from a Faithful Fool

Rev. R. Tony Ricard, M.Th., M.Div.

Two Knights Publishing Company
1835 St. Roch Avenue
New Orleans, Louisiana 70117

First Edition 2010

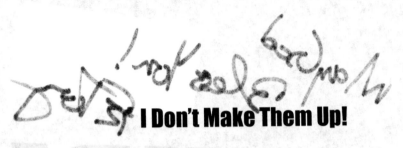

I Don't Make Them Up!

Printed in the United States of America

For more information about Two Knights Publishing Co. or KnightTime Ministries, please visit

www.**FatherTony**.com

All Scriptural quotations are from the New American Bible.

Book edited by Cynthia Capen and Andrew Lopez
Contributing Photographers - Paula Burch-Celentano & Alexis Robinson
Cover by Bjorn Jon Madrid, Graphic Designer

ISBN-13:   978-0-9793157-3-2
ISBN-10:   0-9793157-3-5

This book is dedicated
to the Men Who Help to Keep Me Faithful to God

My Priest Mentor
Rev. Joseph A. Brown, SJ

My Childhood Priests and Pastors

Rev. Msgr. Lanaux Rareshide

Rev. Victor Cohea

Rev. Quentin Moody

Rev. Msgr. Thomas Glasgow

Rev. Ferdnand Cheri, OFM

My "Council of Clergy Advisors"

Rev. Msgr. Robert Guste

Rev. J. Derran Combs, OFM

Rev. Peter Weiss, SSJ

Rev. Mr. Melvin Jones

Rev. Mr. Uriel Durr

Rev. Msgr. Doug Doussan

Rev. John Ciseweski

Rev. Anthony Bozeman, SSJ

Rev. Mr. Jesse Watley

Rev. Mr. Brian Gabriel

to the Men Who Provide the Fuel to My Foolishness

Glenn Chenier

Steve Dooley, IV

Corey Ricard

Chris A. Quest, II

Denzel J. Millon

Tracy McElveen

Justin Smith

Albert Lopez

Dernattel Foucher

Daniel H. Green

Andrew Lopez

Blair K. McDonald

Jared Landry

Tevin Clausen

Jessie Turner

Ernesto Ramirez

to the Men Who Inspire Me to Be Me

Rodney J. Ricard (My Dad)

Jesse Manibusan

Paul Florez

Kevin J. Ricard (My Brother)

Mike Patin

Ansel Augustine

In the Memory of the Men Who Paved the Way for Me to Be a Priest

Most Rev. Harold R. Perry, SVD, First African-American Bishop
in Modern Times and My Pastor at Our Lady of Lourdes Parish

Rev. Aubry Osborne, First African-American Priest
for the Archdiocese of New Orleans

Introduction

"Consider your own calling, brothers and sisters. Not many of you were wise by human standards, not many were powerful, not many were of noble birth. Rather, God chose the foolish of the world to shame the wise and God chose the weak of the world to shame the strong, and God chose the lowly and despised of the world, those who count for nothing, to reduce to nothing those who are something, so that no human being might boast before God." (1 Corinthians 26-29)

More times than not, folks who love their God and love their Church have been called "fools" by those who just don't understand. Yet, "Crazy Fools" are definitely those whom we should strive to be in the eyes of the world. For, it is the foolish that God uses to shame the wise.

We are all invited by God to focus on what it means to be a "fool for the Lord." Through these entertaining Reflections, Stories and Jokes, we can find true joy in the midst of life's great struggles. For spiritual laughter conveys joy to the entire human family, uplifts our souls and energizes our evangelical spirit!

I have been blessed to preach and teach before thousands and thousands of people. In my presentations and homilies, I often use humor to express the love of God, uplift the downtrodden, and celebrate who we are as God's Beloved. Although I can take credit for many of the stories that I've used, I really have to admit that I've "appropriated" most of them from other speakers and presenters. I've especially been known to "borrow" jokes from my ministerial inspirations: Jesse Manibusan, Mike Patin and Paul Florez. Each of them are phenomenal speakers in their own rights.

Once I "digest" a story, I try to retell it in an exciting new way. To make the story more realistic, I usually place myself in it. It is amazing how many folk actually believe that the stories are true.

The Reflections, Stories and Jokes that are included in this book are a collection from many sources. Most of them are jokes that I have heard or have been sent by friends and family. I especially want to thank Carl Kluttz and Norman Howard for the many jokes they have sent to me through the years.

Now you know why at the end of almost all of the jokes that I tell, I say, "I Don't Make Them Up! I Just Repeat Them!"

May this book lift your Spirit so that you too may long to be a Fool for the Lord!

Rev. R. Tony Ricard, M.Th., M.Div.

Table of Contents

SECTION ONE
"In the Beginning...."

"God looked at
everything
He had made,
and
He found it
very good."

Genesis 1:31

My Version of the Creation Story
an Introduction

Back in 1990, I got to hear Dr. William Henry Cosby, Jr., the infamous educator, or "Bill Cosby" as we commonly know him, tell a version of the Creation Story that was insightful and yet quite funny.

He has the rare ability to take a familiar story or life experience and share it with his audiences in such a way that only makes them laugh, but has them thinking a bit deeper.

After hearing Bill Cosby's version of the Creation Story, I tried to retell the story in the same manner that he did. Suddenly, I realized that I was no Bill Cosby. No one can really tell a Bill Cosby story quite like he does.

Soon, I realized I had to develop my own version of the Creation Story using my own vision, and combining it with a little flavor of my own.

So, I did.

The most impressionable stories told involve audience participation, I know this first-hand from being a certified elementary school teacher in New Orleans.

So, I incorporated interactive motions from an activity that I learned while directing a youth retreat with the innovative Mike Patin.

He served as the Director of Youth Ministry for the Archdiocese of New Orleans for many years. In a very real way, Mike is responsible for beginning my ministry as a national speaker. He really deserves the credit for presenting "The Aura that is Tony" worldwide.

When I was a seminarian, Mike was the first to recognize my blessings and gifts for Youth Ministry. Not long after I entered the seminary, Mike was beginning to recommend me for speaking engagements and retreats. I was invited to be the keynote speaker for the 1992 Diocesan Youth Conference in the Diocese of Lake Charles, Louisiana. That was my very first time as a keynote speaker.

While directing a retreat with Mike, I watched him engage the youth in an activity that he called, "The Magic Go." This is how it worked. Every time he said the word, "Go," he would direct the kids to complete a series of motions; slaps, claps and even finger snaps.

When I developed my version of the Creation Story, I incorporated Mike's "Magic Go" command with my humorous rendition of the story. But, instead of using the word, "Go," to signal the interactive motions, I switched it to the word, "Boom!"

Every time the youth hear the word, "Boom," in the Creation Story, they are directed to do the following:

1. Slap their legs (once)

2. Clap their hands (once)

3. Snap their fingers (twice)

4. Yell, "Whoop, there it is!"

Adding "Boom!" to the story really brought it to life!

To this day, I thank Bill Cosby and Mike Patin for inspiring me to create one of my most successful stories.

It sure is good!

The Creation Story
Inspired by God - Written by Moses and Interpreted by Fr. Tony

Once upon a time, or really, "In the Beginning,"[1]
God was in Heaven and He said to Himself, "Self...."
(Hey, there wasn't anybody else to talk to!)

"Self, I'm feeling kinda lonely. So, I think that I'll make me something."

On the **First Day,** the Lord said, "Let there be Light!"

Boom!

And the Angels cried out, "Whoop There It Is!"[2]

And there it was. And the Light was everywhere.

And when the Lord looked upon the Light, His Heart was filled with Love.

So, He looked upon the Light and He said,
"Mmm, Mmm, Mmm, this sure is good!"

Well, that was the First Day.

On the **Second Day**, when the Lord got up, His Heart was filled with Love.
He loved Him some Light.

But, He realized that there was one small problem. "It don't do anything!"

The Light was like "Hey,.... I'm the Light. That's what I do.... I do Light!"

---

[1]Genesis Chapters 1-3

[2]"Whoop There It Is" was the catch phrase made popular in a 1993 Hip- Hop song by Tag Team. The literal translation is "Look, Honey, it's over there!"

So, the Lord decided that He would make something that just might do something.

So, on the Second Day the Lord created the Sky and the Firmament.

Boom!

And the Angels cried out, "Whoop There It Is!"

And, there they were!

And the Light was doing the Light thing. The Sky was doing the Sky thing and the Firmament was....

(Well, who really knows what the Firmament really was. What ever it was....
    it was the potential from which everything else came into being.)

But, whatever it was....the Lord looked upon the Light, the Sky, and the Firmament and He said, "Mmm, Mmm, Mmm, this sure is good!"

And that was the Second Day.

On the **Third Day**, the Lord got up, and His Heart was filled with Love.
    He loved Him some Light, Sky and Firmament.

But, He realized that there was one small problem. "It don't do anything!"

So, on the Third Day, the Lord decided that He would create something that just might do something.

On the Third Day, the Lord created the Dry Land,
    the Dry Earth and the Sea Vegetation.

Boom!

And the Angels cried out, "Whoop There It Is!"

And, there they were!

So, the Mountain was doing the Mountain thing. The Trees were doing the Trees thing and the Grass was doing the Grass thing.

And, the Lord looked upon the Light, the Sky, the Firmament, the Dry Earth, the Earth and Sea Vegetation and He said, "Mmm, Mmm, Mmm, this sure is good!"

And that was the Third Day.

On the **Fourth Day**, the Lord got up and His Heart was filled with Love.
He loved Him some Light, the Sky, the Firmament, the Dry Earth,
the Earth and Sea Vegetation.

But, He realized that there was one small problem.

You see, all this green stuff that He had created didn't know when it was supposed to grow and not grow.

So, He decided to create a system that would tell the green stuff when to grow.

So, on the Fourth Day the Lord reached up into the Sky and He grabbed that thing he called the Light.

He made a great big fiery ball, threw it in the air and called it "the Sun."

Then, He took another piece, made another ball and threw it on the dark side of the Earth and called it "the Moon."

Then, He took a bunch of pieces, chopped them up and threw them in the air. He called them "the Stars."

Boom!

And the Angels cried out, "Whoop There It Is!"

And, there they were!

And, the Lord looked upon the Light, the Sky, the Firmament, the Dry Earth, the Earth and Sea Vegetation, the Sun, the Moon and the Stars and He said, "Mmm, Mmm, Mmm, this sure is good!"

And that was the Fourth Day.

On the **Fifth Day**, when the Lord got up and His Heart was filled with Love.
He loved Him some Light, the Sky, the Firmament, the Dry Earth,
the Earth and Sea Vegetation, the Sun, the Moon and the Stars.

But, He realized that there was one small problem. "It don't do anything!"

(Have you ever tried to play ball with a tree?
After a while, it's going to get boring....for most of us!)

So, on the Fifth Day the Lord decided that He would create something that just might do something.

So, on the Fifth Day, the Lord created Birds in the air and Fish in the water.

Boom!

And the Angels, cried out, "Whoop There It Is!"

And, there they were!

The Birds were doing the Birds thing. The Fish were doing the Fishy thing.

And the Lord looked upon the Light, the Sky, the Firmament, the Dry Earth, the Earth and Sea Vegetation, the Sun, the Moon and the Stars, Birds in the air and Fish in the water and He said, "Mmm, Mmm, Mmm, this sure is good!"

Well, that was the Fifth Day.

On the **Sixth Day**, the Lord got up and His Heart was filled with Love.
He loved Him some Light, the Sky, the Firmament, the Dry Earth,
the Earth and Sea Vegetation, the Sun, the Moon and the Stars,
Birds in the air and Fish in the water.

But, He realized that there was one small problem.

You see, on one-third of this thing that He called the Earth,
"There wasn't anything living."

One-third of the Earth is dry land.

So, the Lord decided that He would create something that could live on the dry land.

So, on the Sixth Day, the Lord created Animals upon the earth and
Creepy Things that live in Trees!

Boom!

And the Angels cried out, "Whoop There It Is!"

And, there they were!

The Elephant was doing the Elephant thing.
The Monkey was doing the Monkey thing.
The Sheep was doing the Sheep thing.
The Tiger was doing the Tiger thing.

(I'm not going to name them all because there was a lot of them.)

But, the Lord looked upon the Light, the Sky, the Firmament, the Dry Earth, the Earth and Sea Vegetation, the Sun, the Moon and the Stars, Birds in the air and Fish in the water, Animals on the Earth and Creepy Things in the Trees and He said, "I ain't done, yet!"

In looking at all that He had created,
        the Lord realized that as much as He loved the things that He had made,
        the problem was that none of them had the ability to love Him back.

The Lord wanted to create a creature that could freely choose to love Him back.

So, similar to how the African-American Poet,
        James Weldon Johnson described it, the Lord stepped down out of
space.

He knelt down beside a river like a Mammy kneeling over a baby
        and He scooped up a hand of clay.

From that clay He created a new being and breathed into him the Breath of Life.

He called him "the Adam!"

Boom!

And the Angels cried out, "Whoop There It Is!"

And, there he was!
        Adam, standing there in all his glory!

Then the Lord looked at Adam and said, "You the Man!"

To which Adam thumped his chest and exclaimed, "I'm the Man!"

The Lord said, "Adam, you have dominion over the whole earth!"

To which Adam thumped his chest and exclaimed, "I've got dominion!"

The Lord said, "Whatever name you give something will be its name!"

Adam thumped his chest, again and said, "I've got names!"

Pointing to a big, fat, gray thing with a long nose,
     the Lord asked Adam, "What's that?"

"That looks like an Elephant to me," Adam replied.

And, the Lord said, "Alright Adam, that's an Elephant."

Looking at another animal with a long neck that was eating leaves
     at the top of a tree, the Lord asked, "Hey Adam, what's that?"

To which Adam replied, "Lord, that looks like a Giraffe to me."

And, the Lord said, "Adam, that's a Giraffe."

Then they saw another big, fat, gray thing with a horn on its nose,
     and the Lord asked, "Hey Adam, what's that?"

"That looks like a Rhinoceros to me," Adam replied.

And, the Lord said, "Adam that's a Rhinoceros!"

Then they saw this thing that looked liked a like a combination between an
Elephant and a Rhino.

And, the Lord said, "Adam, what's that?"

To which Adam replied, "Eleph-phino!" (Get it.... "El - Eph - I - No?")

And so, the Lord said, "Adam man, you just go and have a good time!"

So, Adam set out to enjoy the Earth. He was loving being "the Man."

But, about midway through the afternoon of the Sixth Day,
        Adam realized that there was one BIG problem.

So, Adam headed up to Heaven to have a talk with God.

When he knocked on the Gates of Heaven,
        the Lord answered and asked him, "Adam, is there a problem?"

"Oh no, Lord," Adam said,
        "I don't mean to complain because I've got it pretty good."

"But, umm....You see, Lord, every night,
        I see Mr. and Mrs. Elephant go home.
Lord, every night, I see Mr. and Mrs. Giraffe go home.
        Lord, even the Rhinoceros has somebody.
        Umm...., you think you could just....hook a Brother up?"

And the Lord, replied by saying, "Adam....Adam....Adam?
        Are you sure you know what you are asking for?
        Why don't you just go to sleep?"

Well, they say that Adam laid down beside that same river.

In order for the Lord to fashion this new creature out of the very same substance
that He created the first one, the Lord stepped down out of space.

He reached down inside of Adam and pulled out a rib.

From that rib, He fashioned a new being.
        And, He breathed into her the Breath of Life.
        He called her "Eve!"

Boom!

And the Angels cried out, "Whoop There It Is!"

And, there she was standing there in "all her glory."

When Adam woke up and opened his eyes,
        that is when she got her official name.

Because, when he saw her standing there by the river, the first thing he said was
"Whoa Man!"

(Get it, Whoa Man....wo----man = Woman!)

Adam looked up to Heaven and he said,
"Lord, You the Man! You the Man!" The Lord smiled down on them and said,
"Ya'll just head out and have a good time!"

As Adam and Eve headed out into the Garden, the Lord looked upon the Light,
the Sky, the Firmament, the Dry Earth, the Earth and Sea Vegetation, the Sun,
the Moon and the Stars, Birds in the air and Fish in the water, Animals on the
Earth, Creepy Things in Trees, Man and Woman, and He said,
"Mmm, Mmm, Mmm, this sure is VERY Good!"

Did you know that at the end of the Sixth Day of Creation, the Lord looked upon
all that He had created, His Heart was filled with Love.

But, He realized that in creating Eve, He had reached the peak of Creation.
Never again would anything be created greater than Man and Woman.

So, instead of declaring that we were good,
the Lord declared that we were "Very Good."

And, that was the Sixth Day.

On the **Seventh Day**, the Lord got up and His Heart was filled with Love.
He loved Him some Light, the Sky, the Firmament, the Dry Earth, the Earth and
Sea Vegetation, the Sun, the Moon and the Stars, Birds in the air and Fish in the
water, Animals on the Earth, Creepy Things in Trees, Man and Woman.

On the Seventh Day the Lord realized that Adam and Eve were already
teenagers, so He took the Seventh Day off.

He knew that He would never rest again!

On the **Eighth Day**, the Lord went looking for His two kids.
He was yelling, "Adam?....Eve?....Where ya'll at?"

Adam turned to Eve and asked,
"Do you think that He could see us behind this tree?"

11

To which Eve replied, "Dummy, He MADE the tree!"

So, Adam stepped out from behind the tree and called out,
"Lord, we're right here."

"What are you doing?, the Lord asked.
"We're hiding?" Adam replied.

"And why were you hiding?," the Lord asked.
"Because we were naked.," Adam said.
"Naked? How did you know that you were naked?," the Lord asked.

Adam tried to explain,
"Well, you know Lord, last night, the Woman that you gave me made
a wonderful meal. It was so delicious. That girl can really cook!"

The Lord asked Adam, "Where did you get the food for the meal?"

Adam replied, "From the tree in the center of the Garden.
The same tree that you told us not to touch."

And the Lord declared,
"Adam, when I created you, I gave you dominion over the whole Earth.
Everything that I created was made for you to enjoy.
But, the only rule that I gave you to live by was simply this;

you could not touch the Tree in the center of the Garden, that Tree will be
forever known as "the Tree of the Knowledge of Good and Evil."

That was it, that was my only rule! But, you had to go and touch my Tree!

Well, guess what? Like all good parents, if you can't live by the rules
in My House, then you have to get out!"

And on that day, the Lord put us out of the Garden
and we have been trying to get back in ever since!

Boom!

And the Angels, cried out, "Whoop There It Is!"

The Eagle Story
an Introduction

When I entered the Seminary back in 1990, I began working towards a Master of Divinity Degree at Notre Dame Seminary in New Orleans.

At the same time, I enrolled at Xavier University of Louisiana to begin working on a Master of Theology Degree through the Institute for Black Catholic Studies.

Although I learned a great deal at Notre Dame, much of what I do now as a speaker and teacher comes from my studies at Xavier University.

My style of preaching, my flare for dramatics, my good looks (wait, that came from my Momma), and even my story telling were all gifts and talents that I was able to refine from Xavier University's program.

The Institute for Black Catholic Studies was truly a focal point of my training and formation for the priesthood.

During a course I took on Catechesis in the African-American Community, I came across a wonderful story about overcoming the tough odds of life. It was a story that I had heard as a child. So, I was delighted to hear it again.

This inspirational story was handed down to us by enslaved Africans and has been told all over the United States and in several different countries.

It is called "The Eagle Story".

As best as I can tell, my version of the Eagle Story can be traced back to a tale from the West African country of Ghana.

The Eagle Story

Once there was a Chicken Farmer, and on his farm he had some Chickens.

One day the Chicken Farmer was talking to his friend and he said, "My friend,
       I've got this problem. You see, my Chicken Farm ain't doing too well."

His friend replied, "I'll tell you what you ought to do. You see, just the other day,
       I was up in the mountain and I spied this great big Eagle.

If you could somehow catch that Eagle, bring her down and put her in a cage,
       people would pay you money to see that Eagle.
       You could call it the Eagle Zoo."

"That's a great idea," the Farmer said, "That's just what I will do."

So early the next morning, he got up and he tucked his eagle-catching net under his arm and headed up the mountain.

But as he climbed up that mountain, the Eagle heard him coming.
       So, she sat up in her nest.

When the Farmer got really close, the Eagle took off flying in the air.

Well, he took his net and threw it on the Eagle trapping her wings.

She immediately plummeted to the ground and died.

       (Because she busted her head on a rock.)

Seeing the dead Eagle, the Farmer panicked and ran down the mountain
       to see his friend.

"I killed the Eagle, Man! I killed the Eagle!" he shouted.

"Did you check the nest?" his friend asked.

       "Well, Maybe there was something in the nest that you could sell."

So, early the next morning the Farmer climbed back up the mountain.

When he got really close to the nest, he reached up and put his hand inside it.
    And, there he found two Eagle eggs.

He grabbed those two eggs and he hurried down the mountain.

    Getting back to his Chicken coop, he rushed inside.

There he looked for the biggest and fattest hen he could find.

He lifted her up, put those eggs down under her and then looked at her and said,
    "Girl, do your thing."

Well, she took her big fat Chicken butt and sat on those eggs.
    And she sat and she sat and she sat.

Before you knew it, one of those eggs began to hatch. Out popped the prettiest,
little brown Eaglet that you could ever want to see.
    (Eaglet is what they call baby Eagles.)

At feeding time, when they would throw the corn to the left and he'd run to the
left to get some corn. And when they would throw the corn to the right, he'd run
to the right to get the corn.

He was just as happy as ever being a Chicken.

Soon, the other egg began hatch and out popped another little Eaglet.

Well, when they would throw the corn to the left and he'd go get the corn.

And when they would throw the corn to the right, he'd walk over
    and get some more stupid corn.

But, after a while he was getting tired of all this Chicken....mess.

Soon, he began spending most of his days lying out in the field
    looking up at the clouds.

One day, while he was staring at the clouds,
    he spied this great big brown dot in the sky.

That dot was going 'round and around and around.
 He began to realize that this dot was a bird.

 A great big bird.

When he looked up, that bird flew down and landed right beside him.

So, he looked up at that bird and that bird looked down at him.
 He looked up and the bird, and the bird looked down at him.

He looked up at the bird and he said, "Hey, who are you?"
 And the bird replied, "I am an Eagle. And, just who are you?"

"Well," the Eaglet said, "They call me Turk, and I am a Chicken."

"Turk" the big Eagle said,
 "You're not a Chicken. You're an Eagle!"

Turk looked up at him and said, "Let me tell you one thing:

My Momma was a Chicken.
My Daddy was a Chicken.
I live on a Chicken Farm.
I do Chicken things and I eat Chicken food.

I'm telling you.
 I'm a Chicken!"

"Let me tell YOU something," said the Eagle.

"Your Momma was an Eagle, the Queen of all the birds.
 When your Momma took off to fly all of the other birds would stop to
 watch her soar.

And, your Daddy, boy....,
 your Daddy was an Eagle, the King of all the birds.

Your Daddy ran all of the Birds' Meetings.
 When your Daddy spoke, everybody listened.

I'm telling you, Boy....you're an Eagle."

16

Turk looked up at him and said, "Let me tell you one thing:

My Momma was a Chicken.
My Daddy was a Chicken.
I live on a Chicken Farm.
I do Chicken things and I eat Chicken food.

I'm telling you.
        I'm a Chicken!"

"Well," that Eagle thought to himself,
        "Tell you what I'm gonna do. I'll take him to the top of the tree."

So he put his big brown wing around Turk and flew up him to the top of the tree.

From the top of the trees, he looked at Turk and he said, "Jump!"

Turk looked up and him and said, "You must be crazy!
        I have told you before, I am a Chicken.
        Now I might make it from the coop to the fence, but that's about it."

The Eagle looked at Turk and said,
        "I've told you before, you are an Eagle. So, Jump!"

And Turk said, "Let me tell you one thing:

My Momma was a Chicken.
My Daddy was a Chicken.
I live on a Chicken Farm.
I do Chicken things and I eat Chicken food.

I'm telling you.
        I'm a Chicken!"

The Eagle once again, thought to himself,
        "Tell, you what I'm gonna do. I'll give him a little push."

So, he snuck up behind Turk and BAM!....
        kicked him right in the butt!

There Turk went, falling towards the ground.

Now when Turk got close to the ground,
he had two things between which he could decided.

He could spread out his little brown wings and try,
or he could bust his head on a rock!

Well, as you guessed, Turk, spread out his wings and voooom!
He took off flying in the air.
Flippin' and a floppin,' and a floppin'
and a flippin', because that's what Eagles do.

He flew back to the top of the tree and said,
"I've got to go tell my brother. I've got to go tell my brother!"
So, Turk flew down onto the Chicken Farm landing right next to his brother.

Turk excitedly said to him, "We're Eagles, Man, we're Eagles!"

His brother looked at Turk and thought to himself, "Turk is going crazy!
I wonder what he has been out there doing?"

Turk said hurriedly,
"This great big Eagle came down and he said that Momma was a Queen.
Daddy was a King. Momma flew, Daddy talked.
We're Eagles, Man, we're Eagles!"

His brother looked at him and said,
"Now Turk, I have told you before:

Our Momma was a Chicken.
Our Daddy was a Chicken.
We live on a Chicken Farm.
We do Chicken things and we eat Chicken food.

I'm telling you, Turk,
we'z Chickens!"

Turk thought to himself,
"Tell you what I am gonna do. I'll take him to the top of the tree."

So, Turk put his little brown arm around his brother and flew up him to the top
of the tree. And when they reached the top of the trees, he looked at his brother
and said, "Jump!"

His brother looked back at him and said,
  "Turk, if you don't get me down off this tree, I'm going to kill you!"

"We're Eagles Man, Jump!" hollered Turk. "Jump!"

And his brother replied, "I have told you before:

Our Momma was a Chicken.
Our Daddy was a Chicken.
We live on a Chicken Farm.
We do Chicken things and we eat Chicken food.

I'm telling you, Turk,
  we'z Chickens!"

So, Turk thought to himself,
  "Tell you what I'm gonna do. I'll give him a little push."

So he snuck up behind his brother and BAM!....
  Kicked him right in the butt
sending his brother soaring towards the ground.

Well, as he got closer and closer to the ground,
  he had two things between which he could decide.

He could spread out his little brown wings and try
  or he could bust his head on a rock!

And as you guessed, when he got close to the ground, BAM!

He died.

And that's how the story ends.

(What do you think, every story has a happy ending?)

You see, the problem was, in the mind of Turk's brother, he was still a Chicken.

And, no matter what people said, and no matter what people did,
until he believed in his heart that he was an Eagle, he'd always be a Chicken.

SECTION TWO
Biblical Jokes

Jesus opened
their minds
to understand
the Scriptures.

Luke 24:45

Creating Adam's Helpmate

Not long after Adam was created, he was walking around the Garden of Eden and realizing that all of the other creatures had beautiful helpmates and wives.

The Monkeys, the Lions and even the Hippopotamuses
        had beautiful female companions with which they could run and play.

Looking at poor helpless Adam, the Lord knew that it was not good for him to be alone. The poor boy would never be able to figure out the tougher issues of life.

Without the help of a mate,
Adam would never understand things like balancing a household's budget or solving the mystery of who put the toy soldiers in the toilet.

So, God decided that he would strike a deal with Adam
        and finally create for him a friend.

"Adam," the Lord said, "I have come up with a plan that will make you very very happy! I have envisioned for you a companion, a helpmate who will be able to fulfill your every need and desire.

This new creature will be faithful, loving, and obedient to you. She will make you feel wonderful each and every day of your life."

Adam was so stunned by God's vision that he yelled out,
        "Lord, that sounds incredible!"

"Well, it is," replied the Lord. "But it doesn't come for free.
In fact, this is someone so special that it's going to cost you both of your arms.

Lord, Adam," sighed, "I can't live without my arms."

"OK, Adam," the Lord answered, "I can make you someone who won't be as good as my first vision. But, she will indeed be a great helpmate to you. She will be able to solve all of your problems. However, it will cost you both of you legs."

"That's a pretty high price to pay, Lord," said Adam.

" Ummm Lord, how much could I get for a rib?"

21

Eve's Side of the Story (Rated PG 13)

After three weeks in the Garden of Eden, God came to visit Eve.
"So, how is everything going?" inquired God.

"It is all so beautiful, God," she replied. "The sunrises and sunsets are breathtaking, the smells, the sights, everything is wonderful, but, I have just one problem.

It's these breasts you have given me. The middle one pushes the other two out and I am constantly knocking them with my arms, catching them on branches and snagging them on bushes. They're a real pain."

Eve went on to tell God that since many other parts of her body came in pairs, such as her legs, arms, eyes, and her ears. So, she felt that having only two breasts would help make her body more "symmetrically balanced."

"That's a fair point," replied God, "But it was my first shot at this, you know. I gave the animals six breasts, so I figured that you needed only half of those, but, I see that you are right. I will fix it up right away."

And God reached down, removed the middle breast and tossed it into the bushes.

Three weeks passed and God once again visited Eve in the Garden of Eden.
"Well, Eve, how is my favorite creation?"

"Just fantastic," she replied, "Except for one oversight. You see, all the animals are paired off. The ewe has a ram and the cow has her bull. All the animals have a mate except me. I feel so alone."

God thought for a moment and said, "You know, Eve, you are right. How could I have overlooked this? You do need a mate and I will immediately create a man from a part of you. Let's see, where did I put that useless boob?"

(My best friend, Cathy, thinks that this makes more sense than all that stuff about the rib!)

Gonna Have a Wife

One day, at Catechism, they were teaching how God created everything,
   including human beings.

Little Johnny seemed especially intent when they told him
   how Eve was created out of one of Adam's ribs.

Later in the week, his mother noticed him lying down
      as though he were sick, and she said,
      "Johnny, what is the matter?"

Little Johnny responded,
      "I have pain in my side."
      "I think I'm going to have a wife."

Thou Shalt Not Kill

A CCD Teacher was trying to explain the Ten Commandments
   to her five and six year olds students.

After explaining that the commandment "Honor thy father and thy mother,"
   means that we should listen to our parents and always be nice to them,
   she asked her class if there is a commandment
   that teaches us how to treat our brothers and sisters.

Without missing a beat, Little Johnny answered,
   "It has got to be 'Thou shall not kill!'"

The 17ᵗʰ Chapter of Mark

At the conclusion of his Homily,
     Father Tony gave his congregation a little homework to do.

"Next weekend, I will be preaching about the Ninth Commandment.
     To help you better understand my homily,
     I want you all to go home and read the 17ᵗʰ Chapter of Mark."

The following Sunday,
     Father Tony stood in the pulpit
     and ask everyone who read the 17ᵗʰ Chapter of Mark to raise their hands.

He was surprised when almost everyone in the church put their hands in the air.

"My Brothers and Sisters," he began,
     "the Ninth Commandment says,
     'Thou Shalt Not Bear False Witness Against Thy Neighbor.'
     That means that we should not lie.

     As I continue, I guess that I should tell you that
     the Gospel of Mark only has 16 Chapters."

(You could have heard a pin drop as he continued his sermon on lying!)

A New Bible Quiz!

Where is baseball in the Bible?
"In the big-inning, God created…" (Gen. 1:1)

Why did Adam and Eve become mathematicians?
God told them to be fruitful and multiply.

Why couldn't Cain please his parents?
He just wasn't Abel.

Why didn't Pharaoh stop swimming when the plagues started?
He was in da Nile.

How could people tell David was a shepherd when he fled from Saul?
He went on the lam.

Which prophet was most likely to wear contact lenses?
"Eyes – aiah" (Isaiah)

Why did Jesus perform His first miracle at Cana?
His mother "whined" about it.

What happened at Samson's last temple performance?
He brought down the house.

What did Zacchaeus use on his bulletin board?
Tax

What was Boaz before he married?
Ruthless

Who was the greatest financier in the Bible?
Noah: He was floating his stock while everyone else was in liquidation.

Who was the greatest female financier in the Bible?
Pharaoh's daughter:
She went down to the bank of the Nile and drew out a little prophet.

What excuse did Adam give to his sons as to why they did not lived in Eden?
Your mother ate us out of house and home.

Which servant of God was the most flagrant lawbreaker in the Bible?
Moses: He broke all 10 commandments at once.

Who is the greatest baby-sitter mentioned in the Bible?
David: He rocked Goliath to a very deep sleep.

What kind of cars are in the Bible?
Hondas: The Apostles were all in one Accord.

Which area of Palestine was especially wealthy?
The area around Jordan: The banks were always overflowing.

Which Bible character had no parents?
Joshua: He was the son of Nun.

Why didn't they play cards on the Ark?
Because Noah was standing on the deck.

Why is it a sin for a woman to make coffee?
It's in the Bible. It says . . . "Hebrews."

Bonus Question:

What do they call Bishops in Germany?
German Shepherds

A Response of Biblical Proportions

As the new Pastor in town, Fr. Jim decided that he would visit the homes of as many families as he could so that he could become familiar with the community.

Each day, he would stop by a different home
and on most days, he was welcomed in by the families.

On one particular Saturday night, all seem well as he walked up to the porch of one of his elderly parishioner's home.

Although it was obvious that someone was home, no one came to the door even though he had knocked several times on the door.

Finally, he took out his card,
wrote on the back "Revelation 3:20" and stuck it in the door.

The next day, as he was counting the collections from Sunday's Mass,
he found his card in the collection plate.

Below his message was the notation "Genesis 3:10."

Revelation 3:20 reads:

"Behold, I stand at the door and knock.
If anyone hears my voice, and opens the door,
(then) I will enter his house
and dine with him,
and he with me."

Genesis 3:10 reads:

"I heard you in the garden;
but I was afraid,
because I was naked,
so I hid myself."

The Attitudes of Be!

Jesus took his disciples up on the mountain
and gathered them around Him.

And He taught them, saying:

> *Blessed are the poor in spirit,*
> *Blessed are the meek,*
> *Blessed are the merciful,*
> *Blessed are you who thirst for justice,*
> *Blessed are you who are persecuted,*
> *Blessed are the peacemakers[3]*

And Simon Peter said, "Do we have to write this stuff down?"

And Philip said, "Will this be on the test?"

And John said, "I'm sorry. Would you mind repeating that?"

And Andrew said, "John the Baptist's disciples don't have to learn this stuff!"

And Matthew said, "Huh?"

And Judas said, "What does this have to do with real life?"

Then, one of the Pharisees, an expert in the law said,
"I don't see any of this in your syllabus.
Do you have a lesson plan? Is there a summary?
Where is the student guide?
Will there be any follow-up assignments?
How will this affect the bell curve?"

And Thomas, who had missed the sermon,
came to Jesus privately and said,
"Did we do anything important on yesterday?"

And Jesus wept.

---

[3]The Beatitudes - Matthew 5:1-12

Dirt

One day,
God was sitting in Heaven having a deep discussion with a noted scientist.

The scientist says to God,
      "Lord, we don't need you anymore.
      Science has finally figured out a way to create life out of nothing.

      In other words, we can now do what you did 'in the beginning'."

"Oh, is that true?
      Tell me...."
            replies God.

"Well," says the scientist,
      "we can take dirt and form it into the likeness of you
      and breathe life into it, thus creating man."

"Well, that's interesting." God replies, "Why don't you show Me."

So the scientist bends down to the Earth
      and starts to mold the soil.

"Oh no, no, no...."
      interrupts God.

      (I love this...)

      "Get your own dirt!"

The Bible and Business

Once there was a man who had been in business for many, many years. After a long struggle, his business was going down the drain. Because of his troubles, he was seriously contemplating suicide because he doesn't know what to do.

He decided to go visit his parish priest to seek his advice. After pouring out his heart to his pastor, he asked the priest what should he do.

This is what the Pastor told him to do:
> Take a beach chair and a Bible and put them in your car.
> Drive down to the edge of the ocean and go to the water's edge.
> Take the beach chair out of the car, sit on it
> and take the Bible out and open it up.
>
> The wind will rifled the pages for a while
> and eventually the Bible will stay open at a particular page.
> Read the Bible and it will tell you what to do.

So, the man did as he was told.

> He placed a beach chair and a Bible in his car
> and drove down to the beach.
> He sat on the chair at the water's edge and opened the Bible.
> The wind did indeed rifle the pages of the Bible
> and then his Bible stopped at a particular page.

He looked down at the Bible and saw what he has to do.

Three months later the man and his family came back to see the Priest. The man was wearing a $1,000 Italian suit. His wife was all decked out with a full-length mink coat and their child was dressed in beautiful silk.

The man handed the Priest a thick envelope full of money and told him that he wants to donate this money to the church in order to thank the Priest for his wonderful advice.

The Priest was very delighted. He asked the business man what advice in the Bible brought this good fortune to him.

To which the man replied, "Chapter 11."

A Wise Guy

Once there was a religious lady that had to do a lot of traveling for her business, so she did a lot of flying. Since flying made her very very nervous, so she always took her Bible along with her to read. It helped relax her on the long fights.

One time, she was sitting next to a skeptical man. When he saw her pull out her Bible, he gave a little chuckle and smirk and went back to what he was doing.

After awhile, he turned to her and asked, "You don't really believe all that stuff in there do you?"

The lady replied, "Of course I do. It is the Bible."

He said, "Well, what about that guy that was swallowed by that whale?"

She replied, "Oh, Jonah. Yes, I believe that. It is in the Bible."

He asked, "Well, how do you suppose he survived all that time inside the whale?"

The lady said, "Well, I don't really know. I guess when I get to heaven, I will ask him."

"What if he isn't in Heaven?" the man asked sarcastically.

"Then you can ask him," replied the lady.

SECTION THREE
Prayerful Jokes

If you remain in Me
and My Words
remain in you,
ask for whatever
you want
and
it will be done for you.

John 15:7

The Best Way To Pray

A priest, a minister and a guru sat discussing the best positions for prayer, while a telephone repairman worked nearby.

"Kneeling is definitely the best way to pray," the priest said.

"No," said the minister.
"I get the best results standing with my hands outstretched to Heaven."

"You're both wrong," the guru said.

"The most effective prayer position is lying down on the floor."

The repairman couldn't contain himself any longer...

"Hey, fellas," he interrupted.

"The best prayin' I ever did was
when I was hangin' upside down from a telephone pole."

Knocking Out Those Hail Mary's

Not too long ago, Our Lady Star of the Sea Church in New Orleans was working hard on renovating and restoring a major light fixture that was the focal point in its 70-feet-high dome. In order to repair the fixture, the restoration company installed scaffolding that took up much of the center of the church. It stretched all the way up to the center of the dome.

Like most Catholic churches, Our Lady Star of the Sea is blessed to have its share of really prayerful folks. At any given Mass, there are at least four or five old ladies who will be working their rosary beads for the entire Mass.

In fact, if you don't have old ladies working those beads,
        your church really ain't Catholic.

Well, one day, as the artist was working on the light fixture, one of the old ladies came into church, knelt down in the front pew and began to recite her rosary.

She was working those beads like a champion,
        knocking out those "Hail Mary's."

As she worked those beads, the artist decided to mess with her.
        In the middle of her "Hail Mary's,"
        he leaned down and yelled to her, "Hello down there!"

Well, when that old lady looked up, she didn't see anybody.

So, she went right back to saying her "Hail Mary's," knocking out those beads.

So, once again, he leaned down from his high perch and yelled down,
        "Hello down there!"

But, when that old lady looked up, she didn't see anybody. So, she went right back to saying her "Hail Mary's," knocking out those beads.

Well, this time, the artist decided that he would really mess with her.
        He leaned down and yelled out, "It's me! Jesus!"

To which the old lady responded,

Hush Up! I'm talking to ya Momma!"

God, Can I Have a Penny?

One day, while deep in prayer,
a young man was trying to understand the nature of God.

So, he looked up to Heaven and asked the Lord,
"God, how long is a million years to you?"

God answered,
"My Son, to Me, a million years is like a minute."

Then the man asked,
"God, how much is a million dollars to you?"

And, God replied,
"My Son, to Me, a million dollars is like a penny."

Finally, the man asked,
"God, could you give me a penny?"

And, God says,
"In a minute."

Poor Joe

The other day, a guy named Joe found himself in dire straights.

His business had started to go bust and he found himself in serious financial trouble. He was so desperate that he decided to pray for help.

"Oh Lord, please help me," Joe prayed.

"I've lost my business and if I don't get some money, I'm going to lose my house as well. Lord, if you could, please let me with the lottery."

Later that night, the lottery winners were announced
and poor Joe was not a winner.

So, Joe, once again, looked up and prayed.

"Oh Lord, please let me win the lottery! I've lost my business, my house is gone and soon, I'm going to lose my car, too."

Again, the nightly report of lottery winners came out and Joe still did not win.

Once again, he prayed.

"Oh, Lord, why have you forsaken me?? I've lost my business,
lost my house and now, I've lost my car. My wife and children are starving.

I don't often ask you for help and I have always been a good servant to you.

PLEASE just let me win the lottery this one time
so that I can get my life back in order ... "

Suddenly, there was a blinding flash of light as the Heavens opened
and Joe was confronted by the voice of the Lord Himself.

"Joe," The Lord said, "You have to at least meet me half way.
Could you at least go and buy a ticket?"

Let Go and Let God

A man was walking in the mountains just enjoying the scenery when he stepped too close to the edge of the mountain and started to fall.

In desperation, he reached out and grabbed a limb of a gnarly old tree hanging onto the side of the cliff.

Full of fear, he assessed his situation.

He was about 100 feet down a shear cliff and about 900 feet from the bottom of the canyon below. If he slipped again, he was definitely going to die.

Filled with fear, he looked up and yelled, "Help me!"

But, there was no answer.

Again and again he cried out for help, but no one answered.

Finally he yelled, "Is anybody up there? "

A deep voice replied, "Yes, I'm up here."

"Who is it?"

"It's the Lord."

"Can you help me?"

"Yes, I can help. Have faith in me."

"Lord, please help me!"

"Let go."

Looking around the man became full of panic. "What?!?!"

"Have faith in me. Let go. I will catch you."

To which the man looked up and yelled out,
"Uh... Is there anybody else up there?"

Praise the Lord! Praise the Lord! Praise the Lord!

Once, there was a very devoted Christian lady who lived next door to an Atheist. Every day, when the lady prayed, the atheist guy could hear her. At the end of her prayers, she would always shout, "Praise the Lord."

Every time the Atheist heard her shouting, "Praise the Lord," He'd think to himself, "That old lady is nuts!; praying all the time like that. Don't she know there ain't no God?"

Many times while she was praying, he would go to her house and harass her, shouting at her, "Lady, why do you pray all the time? Why do you shout, 'Praise the Lord?' Don't you know there ain't no God?"

All she would do is look at him, make the Sign of the Cross, and then keep on praying.

One day, the Old Lady found herself in serious need. It was the end of the month, she had run out of food, and she had no money to go out and buy food.

So, as usual, she took it to the Lord in prayer and began to thank the Lord already for what he was going to do. Shouting, "Praise the Lord!" in her excitement.

As usual, the Atheist was annoyed by her praying and thought to himself. "Hmph....Well, this time I'll fix her."

So, he went to the grocery store, bought a whole bunch of groceries, took them to that Old Lady's house, put them on the front porch, rang the door bell and then hid in the bushes to see what she would do.

Well, when she opened that front door and saw those groceries,
    she immediately began to praise the Lord
    with all her heart, all her mind and all her soul;
    she was jumping all about,
    singing Songs of Praise
    and shoutin' everywhere!

"Praise the Lord! Praise the Lord! Praise the Lord!"

The Atheist then jumped out of the bushes and laughingly told her,
    "You crazy old Woman! God didn't buy you those groceries,
    I bought those groceries!"

When she heard that, she broke out and started running down the street,
    shouting even louder,
    "Praise the Lord! Praise the Lord! Praise the Lord!"

When the shocked Atheist finally caught her, he asked what was her problem.

She said, "I knew it! I knew It! Praise the Lord! I knew it!"

"You knew what?," he asked.

"I knew the Lord would provide me with some groceries," she shouted.

    "But, I didn't know he was gonna make the Devil pay for them!"

    "Praise the Lord! Praise the Lord! Praise the Lord!"

St. Jude Candles

Mrs. Jackson was walking down Canal Street in New Orleans
when she met up with Father Tony.

"Good morning," Father said.
"Didn't I marry you and you husband about six years ago?"

"Yes, Father. You certainly did preside at our wedding." she replied.

"Do ya'll have any children, yet?" he asked.

"No, not yet." she said.

"Well, next week, I am going to be preaching for the St. Jude Novena over
at Our Lady of Guadalupe Church on North Rampart Street.
If it's alright with you, I'll light a St. Jude Candle for you and your husband."

"Thank you, Father," she said as they continued on their way.

Quite a few years later, Father Tony ran into Mrs. Jackson again.
"Well, Mrs. Jackson, how are you doing these days?" he asked.

"I am doing well." she replied.

Father then asked her, "Do ya'll have any children, now?"

"Oh yes, Father!" she said.
"Since I last saw you, we've had eleven children:
three sets of twins, and five singles."

"My Lord," Father Tony replied.
"You guys have been busy! Where is Mr. Jackson?"

She responded,
"He over by St. Jude, trying to blow out that darn candle!"

SECTION FOUR
Ministry Jokes

There is an appointed
time for everything,
and a time for every
affair under the
heavens....

A time to weep,
and a time to laugh;
a time to mourn,
and a time to dance.

Ecclesiastes 3:1.4

It's A Miracle

The other day, Fr. Tony was in the Sacristy preparing for Mass.

As he hurried to get everything ready for the service,
    one of the altar servers rushed in and began to yell.

    "Father, Father, Father!" he said.

"WHAT?" replied the priest.

"Let me tell you what I just saw," he said.

"Well, what did you see?" replied the priest.

"Well, I saw this man coming into church.
    He was walking with crutches.

    He walked up to the Holy Water Font
    and he rubbed some Holy Water on his leg.

    Then, he took his crutch and threw it in the air.

Next, he took some more Holy Water and rubbed it on his other leg.
    And, once again, he threw his other crutch into the air."

"That's a miracle!" exclaimed the priest.

"Where is that man?" he asked.

To which the boy replied,
    "He's flat on his butt, right by the Holy Water!"

42

Two Trouble Makers

A young couple were blessed by God with two mischievous sons, ages 8 and 10.

They were always getting into trouble. They caused trouble at school, in church and even at home. It seemed that no amount of punishment could stop them from causing all kinds of problems.

The boys' mother heard that Father Tony was often successful in disciplining children, so she asked if he would speak with her boys. Father agreed and asked to see them individually.

So, the next morning, the mother brought their 8-year-old in first.

As the boy entered his office, the priest greeted him, with a joyful, "Good morning." But, the only response that the boy would give was a grunt.

So, he greeted him again. And, once again, the boy would only grunt.

Realizing that he would soon get angry if the boy kept grunting, the priest decided to change his approach and simply ask the boy about his understanding of God.

So, the priest looked at the boy and asked, "Where is God?"

To which the boy looked up but didn't reply.

So, Father Tony said it louder, "Where is God?"

But the boy still didn't reply.

So, he yelled at the top of his voice, "WHERE IS GOD?!"

The boy was so scared that he immediately jumped up from the chair, ran out of the rectory and headed to his home. Once he arrived home, he ran into his room, hid in the closet and covered up with a blanket.

When his older brother found him in the closet, he asked, "What happened?"

The younger brother, gasping for breath, replied: "We are in real BIG trouble this time! God is missing, and they think we did it!"

The Lie Competition

While walking down the street, one day,
    Father Tony noticed a group of boys who were standing around a dog.

Now, every time he would look in their direction, the boys would start to giggle.

Fearing that they were going to harm the dog, Fr. Tony approached them and
said sternly, "Gentlemen, I know that you are not planning to hurt that dog."

One of the boys looked up and replied, "Oh no, Father.
    We're not going to hurt the dog. We love the dog. And, that's why we've
    decided that whoever could tell the biggest lie could have the dog."

One of the boys raised his hand and said, "My daddy is Michael Jordan.
    He flies home to play basketball with me on every Sunday!"

To which the group replied, "Nah, nah nah!"

Another boy looked up and said, "Well, my daddy is President Barack Obama
    and I can go anywhere in the country that I want to!"

And, once again, the group replied, "Nah, nah nah!"

A third boy chimed in, "My daddy is Bill Clinton!"
    (All things are possible......)

But, the group still replied, "Nah, nah nah!"

Growing angry at their lies, Father Tony began to scold them for their actions.

"Gentlemen," he said, "Don't you already know that lying is a sin.
    It says it right there in the Bible -
    Thou Shalt Not Bear False Witness Against Thy Neighbor.

    That means that you are not supposed to lie!

    When I was you age, I never told a lie!"

To which one of the boys replied,
    "Give him the dog!"

44

The Coffin Attack!

The other night, my rottweiler, Pepper Louise, and I were out on an evening stroll. As we walked a block from my rectory, we began to pass the entrance gates to the historic St. Roch Cemetery.

Now, normally, I won't walk past those gates at night. I am easily scared!

But, for some reason, Pepper wanted to head in that direction.

As we passed the gates, we suddenly heard a noise coming from behind the walls of the graveyard. "Thump Thump.............Thump Thump...........Thump Thump!"

As the noise got louder, I grew more scared and wondered what could be making the noise. "Thump Thump...............Thump Thump...................Thump Thump!"

However, Pepper was not as curious as I was.

Once she heard the noise, she immediately took off running back to our rectory.

Although she is supposed to be my protection, she wasn't going to be around to see from what I was going to need to be protected!

"Thump Thump......................Thump Thump......................Thump Thump!"

Once she took off running, I took off running, too.
"Thump Thump......................Thump Thump.......................Thump Thump!"

When I look behind us, would you believe that I saw a coffin coming out of the cemetery and heading towards us?

It was standing on it's edge moving in our direction.
"Thump Thump..................Thump Thump...............Thump Thump!"

The quicker we ran, the quicker the coffin began to follow us.
"Thump Thump...........Thump Thump............Thump Thump!"

Once we made it to the rectory, we ran inside and locked the doors.
"Thump Thump....Thump Thump....Thump Thump!"

And, the coffin smashed right through the wooden door.

"Thump Thump....Thump Thump!

So, we ran up the stairs.....
    And the coffin followed us.
        "Thump Thump!"

We ran into my bedroom.....
    And the coffin followed us.
        "Thump Thump!"

We ran into the bathroom....
    And the coffin followed us.
        "Thump Thump!"

So, I opened the medicine cabinet,
    hoping to find something to throw at the coffin.

But all I could find was a bottle of Robitussin.
    "Thump Thump!"

So, in horror, I tossed the bottle at the coffin......
    "Thump!"

And, would you believe
    (just hold ya' breath for this one)

The Coffin Stopped

You know why?....
    Because.....Robitussin can always stop a "Coffin Attack!"[4]

---

[4]It's OK to laugh out loud! Don't act like you didn't see that one coming!

My Beloved Eddie

The other day,
I was sitting in my office when one of our long-time parishioners came in.

As she sat in the chair near my desk, she suddenly burst into tears.

"Miss Lilly, what's wrong?" I asked.

"Well, Father," she sobbed, "I was down at the other church and they refused to bury my Beloved Eddie."

"What do you mean, they refused to bury your Beloved Eddie." I asked.

"You see, Father," she continued,
    "Eddie and I had been together for almost fifteen years.
    Wherever I'd go, Eddie was by my side.
        If I went to the bank, Eddie was there.
        If I went to the grocery store, Eddie was with me.
        Even when I went to the bathroom,
    Eddie would wait outside of the door until I came out."

    But, for the last few days, whenever I'd put water in his dish,
    he wouldn't drink."

"What do you mean, you'd put water in his dish?" I asked.

"O' Father, Eddie was my dog," she replied.

"I'm sorry, Miss Lilly, but we don't bury dogs." I responded.

Well Father," she began to say,
"I was thinking that I would give $10,000 to the priest who would bury my dog."

To which I replied, "Why didn't you tell me that he was a Catholic?"

Shall We Gather at the River

As Father John was completing his homily on temperance,
he concluded by saying,
"If I had all the beer in the world, I'd take it and throw it into the river."

With even greater enthusiasm, he said,
"And if I had all the wine in the world, I'd take it and throw it into the river."

And then finally, he said,
"And if I had all the whiskey in the world, I'd take it and throw it into the river."

As he sat down, the Choir Director stood very cautiously
and announced with a smile,
"Today, our closing song will be number #316: 'Shall We Gather at the River.'"

The Army of the Lord

While welcoming visitors to church, Fr. Joseph noticed a unfamiliar young man entering the church. Shaking his hand, Fr. Joseph told him, "Son, you ought to join the Army of the Lord."

To which the young man replied, "I did, Father, but I'm in the Secret Service!"

Illness and Fatigue

While greeting folks after Mass, Father Tony was asked by one of the parishioners, "Why did they move you from your old parish?"

"I was moved because of illness and fatigue," he replied.

"Illness and fatigue?," the parishioner continued.
"What do you mean you were moved because of illness and fatigue?"

To which Fr. Tony replied, "They were sick of me and I was tired of them!"

Make a Novena

One day, a middle aged gentleman decided to go to Confession.

After walking into the confessional, he knelt down and began to celebrate the Sacrament of Penance.

"Bless, me Father for I have sinned. I stole some lumber."

"What did you do with the lumber?," asked the priest.

"I built a bird house." he replied.

"Pray for the Good Lord to forgive you and say 3 Hail Mary's for penance."
   The priest then asked the man, "Do you have something else to tell me?"

"Yes, Father. With the leftover lumber I put a porch on my house."

"You realize that this is now more serious.
   God gave us a commandment not to steal. For penance, say a Rosary."

The man still appeared to have more to say.

Again, the priest asked, "Do you have something else to tell me?"

"Yes, Father," he continued, "with the leftover lumber I put an extension on my house."

"Now, you have really offended God.
   For penance I want you to make a novena."

The man looked puzzled.
"You do know how to make a novena, don't you?," asked the priest.

To which the man replied,

   "No, I don't Father. But if you've got the plans, I've got the lumber."

Pick Heaven or Hell

One day, while walking down the street, a highly successful executive woman was tragically hit by a bus and she died. Her soul arrived up in heaven where she was met at the Pearly Gates by St. Peter himself.

"Welcome to Heaven," said St. Peter. "Before you get settled in though, it seems we have a problem. You see, strangely enough, we've never once had an executive make it this far and we're not really sure what to do with you."

"No problem, just let me in." said the woman.

"Well, I'd like to, but I have higher orders.
        What we're going to do is let you have a day in Hell and a day in Heaven and then you can choose whichever one you want to spend an eternity in."

"Actually, I think I've made up my mind...
        I prefer to stay in Heaven," said the woman.

"Sorry, we have rules." St. Peter explained.

And with that, St. Peter put the executive in an elevator and it went down-down-down to hell. As the the doors opened, she found herself stepping out onto the putting green of a beautiful golf course.

In the distance was a country club and standing in front of her were all her friends - fellow executives that she had worked with and they were all dressed in evening gowns and cheering for her.

They ran up and kissed her on both cheeks and they talked about old times. They played an excellent round of golf and at night went to the country club where she enjoyed an excellent steak and lobster dinner.

She met the Devil who was actually a really nice guy (kinda cute) and she had a great time telling jokes and dancing.

She was having such a good time that before she knew it, it was time to leave. Everybody shook her hand and waved good- bye as she got on the elevator.

The elevator went up-up-up and opened back up at the Pearly Gates and found St. Peter waiting for her. "Now it's time to spend a day in Heaven," he said.

So she spent the next 24 hours lounging around on clouds, playing the harp and singing with the angels. She had a great time and before she knew it her 24 hours were up and St. Peter came and got her.

"So, you've spent a day in Hell and you've spent a day in Heaven.
      Now, it is time for you to choose your eternal place." he said.

The woman paused for a second and then replied, "Well, I never thought I'd say this, I mean, Heaven has been really great and all, but I think I had a better time in Hell."

So, St. Peter escorted her to the elevator and again she went down-down-down back to Hell. When the doors of the elevator opened, she found herself standing in a desolate wasteland covered in garbage and filth.

She saw her friends dressed in rags, picking up the garbage and putting it in sacks.

The Devil came up to her and put his arm around her.

"I don't understand," stammered the woman, "yesterday I was here and there was a golf course and a country club and we ate lobster and we danced and had a great time. Now all there is a wasteland of garbage and all my friends look miserable."

The Devil looked at her and smiled.
"Yesterday," he said, "we were recruiting you; today, you're on staff."

The Usher

The other day, an elderly woman walked into the local country church.

A friendly usher greeted her at the door and helped her up the flight of steps.

"'Where would you like to sit?," he asked politely.

"The front row, please," she answered.

"You really don'' want to do that," the usher said.

"The pastor is really boring."

"Do you happen to know who I am?," the woman inquired.

"No," he said.

"I'm the pastor's mother," she replied indignantly.

"Do you know who I am?" he asked.

"No," she said.

"Good," he answered and walked away.

A Message to All Teachers and Preachers

"A Sermon Doesn't Have to Be Everlasting To Be Eternal."

Defending Her Honor

A man appears before St. Peter at the Pearly Gates to account for his life.

"Have you ever done anything of particular merit?," St. Peter asks.

"Well, I can think of one thing," the man offers.

> "On a trip to the Black Hills, out in South Dakota,
> I came upon a gang of macho bikers
> who were threatening a young woman.
>
> I directed them to leave her alone, but they wouldn't listen.
>
> So, I approached the largest and most heavily tattooed biker.
> I smacked him on the head, kicked his bike over,
> ripped out his nose ring and threw it on the ground,
> and told him,
> 'Leave her alone now or you'll answer to me.'"

St. Peter was impressed.

"When did this happen?," St. Peter asked.

To which the man replied, "Just a couple minutes ago."

The Internal Revenue Service

"Hello, is this Father Fischer?," the voice on the other line asked.

"Yes, it is." Father Fischer.

"Hi, this is Paul Gordon and I work for the IRS.

If you don't mind, can you please answer a few questions for me?"

"Yes, I can." Father answered.

"Is there a man named Richard Martin in your parish?"

"Yes, there is."

"Do you know this man personally?"

"Yes, I do."

"Did he recently make a $10,000 donation to the church?"

"Yes, he will."

SECTION FIVE
Church Folks Jokes

Jesus said to Simon,
"You are Peter,
and upon this rock
I will build
my Church."

Matthew 16:18

The Pope, Billy Graham & Oral Roberts

The other day, the Pope, Billy Graham, and Oral Roberts all died at the same time and went straight to Heaven.

When St. Peter greeted these three holy men at the Pearly Gates, he realized that there was a major problem.

"Oh, this is terrible!" explained St. Peter. "All three of you guys have done some great things in the name of the Lord, and all three of you will be entering into Heaven.

But, we never expected you guys to show up at the same time. I don't know how to tell you this. Your mansions are not ready."

Let me see if I can get someone to put you up for the night."

So, St. Peter picked up the phone and called down to Hell.

When the devil answered the phone, St. Peter said, "Hey Lou, it's me Pete and I need a favor. You see, I have three guys up here who are all getting into heaven but their rooms aren't ready."

"Do you think that they could spend the night with you?"

Realizing that he hadn't done anything for the Lord in a very long time, the Devil agreed to house the three Holy Men. So, the Pope, Billy Graham, and Oral Roberts headed down to Hell.

After about two hours, the phone in Heaven began to ring. When St. Peter answered the phone, he realized that it was the Devil that was calling.

"Hey Pete, it's me, Lou. Man, you've got to come get these boys. They're causing all sorts of problems.

"What type of problems are they causing?" St. Peter asked.

"Well," the Devil replied, "The Pope is down here forgiving everybody, Billy Graham is down here trying to save everybody, and Oral Roberts has raised enough money to buy air conditioning."

Helping the Church Run Well

The other day, Father Joseph was preaching to his congregation on ways that the parish could improve.

As he preached, his parishioners responded to his words.

"In order for a church to grow, it's got to crawl!"

> And the Church shouted back,
> "Let it crawl, Father. Just let it crawl!"

So, he continued, "In order for a church to grow, it's got to walk!"

> And the people of God shouted back,
> "Let it walk, Father. Just let it walk!"

So, he continued, "In order for a church to grow, it's got to run!"

> And the people of God shouted back,
> "Let it run, Father. Just let it run!"

Then he concluded by saying,
> "In order for a church to run well,
> you've got to put more in the collection!"

> And the people of God shouted back,
> "Let it crawl, Father. Just let it crawl!"

The Pope and the Queen

One day, the Pope visited Queen Elizabeth in London. After the customary greetings, they walked on to the balcony to greet the thousands and thousands of people who had gathered to see them.

While acknowledging her loyal subjects, the Queen turned to the Pope and said, "I bet you that I can make every English and every Anglican person in the crowd go wild with just a wave of my hand."

The Pope said, "No way. You can't do that."

"Watch this!" she replied.

So the Queen waved her hand and every English person in the crowd went crazy. They were waving their hands and shouting, 'God save the Queen!"

Seeing the alluring crowd, the Pope thought to himself, "There is no way that I could allow the Queen to upstage me before all of these people. I have to come up with something to top her little wave!"

After thinking to himself for a short while, he turned to her and said, "I bet you I can make every IRISH and every CATHOLIC person in the crowd go wild, not just now, but for the rest of the week, with just a nod of my head."

To which the Queen replied, "No way!"

So the Pope head-butted her.[5]

_____

[5]I extend my sincere apologies to all our Anglican or Episcopalian brothers and sisters who may have been offended by this joke. But, you do have to admit that it was funny!

58

Money Goes To Church

Over at the Federal Reserve Bank, several dollar bills were about to be retired.

As the moved along the conveyor belt to be burned,
  each began to discuss where life had taken them.

The $20 Bill spoke about traveling all around the world.
  He spent summers in Paris,
  winters in the Bahamas,
  and even had a chance to go to the Carnival in Rio de Janeiro.

  All in all, he had a wonderful life.

The $10 Bill described his journeys around the United States.

  He attended Broadway Plays in New York City.
  He went to movie premieres in Hollywood.
  He even had a chance to go down to the Mardi Gras in New Orleans.

  He, too, had a wonderful life.

"Wow!" said the $1 Bill.
  "Ya'll have really had exciting lives!"

"So tell us," says $20 Bill,
  "where have you been throughout your lifetime?"

The $1 Bill replied,
  "Oh, I've been to the Catholic Church.
  I've been to the Methodist Church.
  I've been to the Baptist Church.
  I've been to the Lutheran Church...."

Th $20 Bill interrupted to ask, "What's a church?"

Pity the Pope

The other day, a priest was sitting on the public bus trying to focus on the many tasks that he needed to accomplish.

As he stared out the window, a drunk man boarded the bus and sat next to him. The priest could smell that the man had been out drinking all night long.

Hoping not to have to hold a conversation with the drunk fellow, the priest continued to look out the window.

The drunk man opened his newspaper and began to read. After a few minutes, he leaned over to the priest and asks, "Father, what causes arthritis?"

Annoyed by the man's drunkenness, the priest thought that he would use this opportunity to teach the man a valuable lesson about life.

"Oh, I'll tell you how you get arthritis." replied the priest.
    "You get it from hanging in the streets, drinking all day long,
    hanging out with loose women! That's how you get arthritis!

"Wow!" the drunk muttered as he returned to reading his paper.

After a while, the priest thought about what he had said. So, he leaned over to the man and apologized.

    "I'm sorry, I didn't mean to come at you so harshly.
    How long have you had arthritis?"

"I don't have it, Father!" the man responded.
    "I was just reading here that the Pope has it."

The Pope and the Lawyer

The Pope and a Lawyer both died
     and found themselves standing at the Pearly Gates.

Each was excited to be in Paradise
     and to be going through Heaven's Orientation program.

In the first phase of the Orientation,
     they received their Heavenly Vestments.

The Pope was given modest white toga, a gold Halo and pair of Wings.
     He was excited to look like all of the other Saints.
The lawyer received a much finer toga. It was made of gold threads
     and was accompanied by a matching pair of wing-tipped shoes.

After receiving their vestments, they were then taken to their new homes.
     The Pope was given a modest little cabin
     while the Lawyer was given an 18-room mansion.

At dinnertime, the Pope receives the standard spaghetti dinner meal
     but the lawyer receives a fine steak meal.

Looking at all that he was receiving and the little that Pope was receiving,
     the lawyer began to suspect that an error has been made.
     So, he asked one of the angels in charge,
     if there had been any kind of mistake.

"This guy was the Pope," he said,
     "and yet, he gets what everyone else gets.
     I was just a lawyer and I'm getting the finest of everything.
     How can that be?"

The angel replied, "It's no mistake, good man.
     Up here, we have lots of Popes,
     but you're the first lawyer we've ever had."

Church Bulletin Bloopers[6]

1. Scouts are saving aluminum cans, bottles, and other items to be recycled. Proceeds will be used to cripple children.

2. Ushers will eat latecomers.

3. The Ladies Bible Study will be held Thursday morning at 10. All ladies are invited to lunch in the Fellowship Hall after the B.S. is done.

4. The Pastor would appreciate it if the ladies of the congregation would lend him their electric girdles for the pancake breakfast next Sunday morning.

5. The audience is asked to remain seated until the end of the recession.

6. Low Self-Esteem Support Group will meet Thursday at 7 to 8:30 PM. Please use the back door.

7. The Pastor is on vacation. Massages can be given to church secretary.

8. The third verse of Blessed Assurance will be sung without musical accomplishment.

9. The Rev. Victor Cohea spoke briefly, much to the delight of the audience.

10. The pastor will preach his farewell message, after which the choir will sing, "Break Forth Into Joy."

11. Next Sunday Mrs. Vinson will be the soloist for the morning service. The pastor will then speak on "Drowning out the Noise of the World."

12. Due to the Associate Pastor's illness, Wednesday's healing services will be discontinued until further notice.

13. Weight Watchers will meet at 7 PM. Please use the large double doors at the side entrance.

---

[6]Who knows if these are from real church bulletins? Does it really matter? There are just plain funny!

14. Remember in prayer the many who are sick of our church and community.

15. The eighth graders will be presenting Shakespeare's Hamlet in the church hall on Friday at 7 PM. The congregation is invited to attend this tragedy.

16. The Archdiocesan Gospel Music Fest was hell at Armstrong Park last weekend.

17. Today's Sermon: "How Much Can a Man Drink?" with hymns from a full choir.

18. On a church bulletin during the pastor's illness: "God is good - Fr. Peter is better."

19. We will have our annual Holy Thursday Potluck Supper: prayers and medication to follow.

20. The outreach committee has enlisted 25 visitors to make calls on people who are not afflicted with any church.

21. Eight new choir robes are currently needed, due to the addition of several new members and to the deterioration of some older ones.

22. The choir invites any member of the congregation who enjoys sinning to join the choir.

23. Don't let worry kill you. Let the Church help.

24. For those of you who have children and don't know it, we have a nursery downstairs.

25. The rosebud on the altar this morning is to announce the birth of Michael Jackson Jones, the sin of Deacon and Mrs. Elton John Jones.

26. This afternoon there will be a meeting in the south and north ends of the church. Children will be baptized at both ends.

27. Tuesday at 4PM there will be an ice cream social. All ladies giving milk please come early.

28.   Wednesday, the Ladies Liturgy Society will meet. Mrs. Jones will sing "Put Me In My Little Bed" accompanied by the choir director.

29.   Thursday at 5PM there will be a meeting of the Little Mothers Club. All wishing to become Little Mothers, please see the pastor in his private office.

30.   This being Easter Sunday, we will ask Mrs. Lewis to come forward and lay an egg on the altar.

31.   Next Sunday, a special collection will be taken to defray the cost of the new carpet. All those wishing to do something on the new carpet will come forward and get a piece of paper.

32.   The ladies of the church have cast off clothing of every kind and they may be seen in the church basement Friday.

33.   A red beans and rice supper will be held on Tuesday evening in the church hall. Music will follow.

34.   At the evening service tonight, the sermon topic will be "What is Hell?" Come early and listen to our choir practice.

35.   The Retreat for New CYO Members will be hell May 10 and 11.

36.   Mrs. Johnson will be entering the hospital this week for testes.

37.   Please join us as we show our support for Amy and Alan who are preparing for the girth of their first child.

38.   The President of the Parish Council unveiled the church's new stewardship campaign by telling the parishioners, "I Upped My Pledge--Up Yours"

39.   Sr. Bertha Belch, a missionary from Africa, will be speaking on Mission Sunday. Come hear Sister Belch all the way from Africa.

40.   The sermon this morning: "Jesus Walks on the Water." The sermon tonight: "Searching for Jesus."

41.   Our youth basketball team is back in action Wednesday at 8 PM in the recreation hall. Come out and watch us kill Christ the King.

42.   Ladies, don't forget the rummage sale. It's a chance to get rid of those things not worth keeping around the house. Don't forget your husbands.

43.   The peacemaking meeting scheduled for today has been canceled due to a conflict.

44.   Smile at someone who is hard to love. Say "Hell" to someone who doesn't care much about you.

45.   Miss Charlene Mason sang "I will not pass this way again," giving obvious pleasure to the congregation.

46.   Next Thursday there will be tryouts for the choir. They need all the help they can get.

47.   Barbara remains in the hospital and needs blood donors for more transfusions. She is also having trouble sleeping and requests tapes of Father Tony's sermons.

48.   Irving Benson and Jessie Carter were married on October 24 in the church. So ends a friendship that began in their school days.

49.   Please place your donation in the envelope along with the deceased person you want remembered.

50.   This evening at 7 PM there will be a hymn singing in the park across from the Church. Bring a blanket and come prepared to sin.

Boudreaux and Lent

Each Friday night after work,
Boudreaux would fire up his outdoor grill and cook a venison steak.

But, all of Boudreaux's neighbors were Catholic....
And since it was Lent, they were forbidden from eating meat on Friday.

The delicious aroma from the grilled venison steaks was causing such a problem
for the Catholic faithful that they finally talked to their priest.

The Priest came to visit Boudreaux, and suggested that he become a Catholic.
After several classes and much study, Boudreaux was finally ready to become a
Catholic.

During the Easter Vigil Mass,
the priest poured Holy Water over him and baptized him
"In the Name of the Father, and of the Son and of the Holy Spirit."

Then the priest said to Boudreaux,
"You were born a Baptist, and raised a Baptist, but now you are a Catholic."

Boudreaux's neighbors were greatly relieved.

That is - until the following Lent. On the first Friday of Lent, the wonderful
aroma of grilled venison filled the neighborhood.

The Priest was called immediately by the neighbors.

As he rushed into Boudreaux's yard, clutching a rosary
and prepared to scold him, he stopped and watched in amazement.

There stood Boudreaux, clutching a small bottle of holy water
which he carefully sprinkled over the grilling meat and chanted:

"You wuz born a deer, you wuz raised a deer, but now you is a catfish."

What is Easter?

The other day, three men died and when to meet St. Peter at the Pearly Gates. St. Peter told the men that before they can enter into Heaven they had answer one question.

So, he turned to the first guy and asked, "My son, what is Easter?"

The man quickly replied, "Oh! That's an easy one. Easter is when when families gather, have a BBQ and light fireworks."

Disappointed, St. Peter kindly explains that is not correct.

So, St. Peter turns to the second guy and asked him, "What is Easter?"

The man replied, "Easter is when Santa Claus leaves presents under the tree and you wake up early in the morning to open them."

Once gain disappointed, St. Peter explains that is not the correct answer to his question.

Not feeling too optimistic, St. Peter turned to the third man and asked, "What is Easter?"

The third man replies, "Well, you see, there was a carpenter from Nazareth named Jesus. He was baptized in the Jordan River then became a preacher. He gathered 12 men to be his disciples and went around the Holy Land teaching and performing miracles. The high priests didn't like Jesus so they had him arrested and handed him over to the Romans to be crucified."

Surprised at the third man's answer, St. Peter interrupts him and tells the other two men to listen to him because he knows what Easter is!

The man then continued, "After his trial, the Romans crucified Jesus outside the city of Jerusalem and they placed his body in a tomb. Then they rolled a huge stone in front of the tomb. Three days later, the stone is rolled away and Jesus comes out of the tomb."

St. Peter could hardly contain his excitement. He was ready to let the third man into Heaven. Until the man continued with saying, "and if he sees his shadow, there will be 6 more weeks of winter."

The Pope Goes to New York

The other day, the Pope traveled to New York City.

After being picked up by a limousine, he looked at the beautiful car and says to the driver, "You know, I hardly ever get to drive. Would you please let me?"

The driver is understandably hesitant and says, "I'm sorry, but I don't think I'm supposed to do that." But the Pope persists, "Please?"

The driver finally lets up. "Oh, all right, I can't really say no to the Pope."

So the Pope takes the wheel, and boy, is he a speed demon! He hits the gas and goes around 100 in a 45 mph zone. A policeman notices and pulls him over.

The cop walks up and asks the Pope to roll down the window. Startled and surprised, the young officer asks the Pope to wait a minute. He goes back to his patrol car and radios the chief.

Cop: Chief, I have a problem.

Chief: What sort of problem?

Cop: Well, you see, I pulled over this guy for driving way over the speed limit but it's someone really important.

Chief: Important like the mayor?

Cop: No, no, much more important than that.

Chief: Important like the governor?

Cop: Way more important than that.

Chief: Like the president?

Cop: More.

Chief: Who's more important than the president?

Cop: I don't know, but he's got the Pope driving for him!

We Need a Priest

The other day, a man was struck by a bus on a busy street in New Orleans.

As he laid dying on the sidewalk, a large crowd of on-lookers gathered around.

"A priest! Could somebody get me a priest?" the man cried.

A policeman tried to help out by checking the folks in the crowd. But, there was no priest, deacon or minister to be found.

"A PRIEST, PLEASE!" the dying man cried out.

As the crowd looked all about, a little old man came forward. He was shabbily dressed and had to have been at least eighty years old.

"Mr. Policeman," says the old man, "I'm not a priest. I'm not even a Catholic. But for fifty years now I've been living behind Our Lady of Lourdes Catholic Church on Napoleon Avenue. Every night I've listened to the Catholic litany. Maybe I can be of some comfort to this man."

The policeman agreed with the old man so he brought him over to where the dying man lay.

The old man gently kneels down, leans over the injured man and says slowly in a solemn voice, "B-4....I-19...N-38....G-54....O-72...."

Catholic Definitions

This information is for Catholics only.
It must not be divulged to non-Catholics.[7]

AMEN: The only part of a prayer that everyone knows.

BULLETIN: Your receipt for attending Mass.

CHOIR: A group of people whose singing allows the rest of the Parish to lip-sync.

HOLY WATER: A liquid whose chemical formula is $H2OLY$.

HYMN: A song of praise usually sung in a key three octaves higher than that of the congregation's range.

RECESSIONAL HYMN: The last song at Mass, often sung a little more quietly, since most of the people have already left.

INCENSE: Holy Smoke!

JESUITS: An order of priests known for their ability to establish colleges with good basketball teams.

JONAH: The original "Jaws" story.

---

[7]The less they know about our rituals and code words, the better off they are.

JUSTICE: When kids have kids of their own.

KYRIE ELEISON: The only Greek words that most Catholics can recognize besides gyros and baklava. (for you non-Catholics it means "Lord have mercy.")

MAGI: The most famous trio to attend a baby shower.

MANGER: Where Mary gave birth to Jesus because Joseph wasn't covered by health insurance. (The Bible's way of showing us that holiday travel has always been rough.)

PEW: A medieval torture device still found in Catholic churches.

PROCESSION: The ceremonial formation at the beginning of Mass consisting of altar servers, the celebrant, and late parishioners looking for seats.

RECESSIONAL: The ceremonial procession at the conclusion of Mass led by parishioners trying to beat the crowd to the parking lot.

RELICS: People who have been going to Mass for so long, they actually know when to sit, kneel, and stand.

TEN COMMANDMENTS: The most important Top Ten list not given by David Letterman.

USHERS: The only people in the parish who don't know the seating capacity of a pew.

Jesus in the Bar Room

The other day, Jesus walked into a bar room and began to greet all of the patrons.

As Jesus sat at the end of the bar and talked with all of the patrons,
    a man with a bad leg walked into the bar.

The man looked down to the end of the bar and noticed the Lord sitting there.

So, he called the bartender over and said,
    "Hey Bartender, you can't tell me that
    Jesus the Christ is sitting at the end of this bar."

"Yes, that's Him." the bartender replied.
    "He comes here regularly to meet the people."

"Well dude," the man answered,
    "please do me a favor and send Him a beer from me!"

So, the bartender brought the beer down to Jesus.
    Jesus looked up and gave the man a little wave
    and then returned to talking with the patrons.

As Jesus was talking with the folks,
    a man with a humped back walked into the bar room.

"Bartender," he said, "you can't tell me that lil Jesus, Son of Mary and Joseph,
    is down at the end of this bar."

"Yes, that's Jesus." the bartender replied.
    "He comes here all of the time."

"Dude," the man responded, "send Him some whiskey from me."

So, the bartender brought the whiskey down to Jesus.
    Jesus looked up and gave the man a little wave
    and then returned to talking with the patrons.

As Jesus continued His conversation with the people in the bar room,
    a man with a withered hand walked into the bar.

When he looked down to the end of the bar, he called to the bartender.

"Hey bartender," he said, "is that ol' J.C. down at the end of this bar?"

"Yes, that's Him." the bartender replied.
> "He comes here all of the time.
> He'll go anywhere He needs to so that He can meet the people."

"Well dude," the man said, "send Him some bourbon from me!"

So, the bartender brought the bourbon down to Jesus.
> Once again, Jesus looked up and gave the man a little wave
> and then returned to talking with the patrons.

Well, after having a fun time with the people
> and after drinking all of those drinks, Jesus was feeling really good.

He decided that on his way out of the bar room He would do something special
> for the three men whom did something special for Him.

So, He walked up to the guy with the bad leg and He said,
> "My friend, for your kindness to me, you're healed!"
> And with one touch from Jesus, the man's leg was healed.

Jesus walked up to the man with the humped back and said,
> "My friend, for your kindness to me, you're healed!"
> And with one touch from Jesus, the hump went down
> and the man was healed.

Then Jesus walked up to the man with the withered hand and said,
> "My friend, for your kindness to me...."

But, before Jesus could continue,
> the man immediately stopped Jesus and said,

> "Lord, please don't touch me.... I'm on Disability!"

Computer Competition: Jesus vs Satan

Jesus and Satan were having an on-going argument about who was better on the computer. They had been going at it for days, and frankly God was tired of hearing all the bickering.

Finally fed up, God said, "THAT'S IT! I have had enough. I am going to set up a computer test that will run for two hours, and from those results, I will judge who does the better job."

So Satan and Jesus sat down at the keyboards and typed away.

They moused.

They faxed.

They emailed.

They emailed with attachments.

They downloaded.

They did spreadsheets!

They wrote reports.

They created labels and cards.

They created charts and graphs.

They did some genealogy reports.

They did every job known to man.

Jesus worked with heavenly efficiency and Satan was faster than hell.

Then, ten minutes before their time was up, lightning suddenly flashed across the sky, thunder rolled, rain poured, and, of course, the power went off. Satan stared at his blank screen and screamed every curse word known in the underworld. Jesus just sighed.

Finally the electricity came back on, and each of them restarted their computers. Satan started searching frantically, screaming: "It's gone! It's all GONE!....I lost everything when the power went out!" Meanwhile, Jesus quietly started printing out all of his files from the past two hours of work.

When Satan noticed Jesus printing His work, he became irate. "Wait!" he screamed. "That's not fair! He cheated! How come He has all His work and I don't have any?"

God just shrugged and said, JESUS SAVES....

SECTION SIX
Priests & Nuns Jokes

You are a
Priest forever
according to the
order of Melchizedek.

Hebrews 7:17

Sister Mary Theresa
and O'Malley's Tavern

On a very cold day in Boston, Sister Mary Theresa and a young man found themselves knee-deep in snow while waiting for the city bus.

"Sister," the young man said, "it is way too cold for us to stand out here waiting for a bus. Maybe we should go across the street into O'Malley's Tavern. We could sit near the front window and watch for the bus."

"Well son," Sister said, "if you think that's a good idea."

So, they headed across the street and into the tavern.

"You know," Sister said, "it's probably not a good idea for us to sit in the window. People shouldn't drive by a Nun in a bar room. Maybe we should get one of those booths in the back. Then you could just keep checking for the bus."

"That's cool," said the young man.

"Sister, while I'm in here, I think that I'll have a beer." he said. "Do you want something? Can I get you a some hot tea, or hot chocolate or coffee?"

"Well son," sister said softly, "while we're in here, why don't you get me a double shot of vodka but have them put it in a plastic cup. I don't want people to know what I am drinking."

"Alright Sister, if that's what you want." chuckled the young man.

As the young man walked up to the bar, he said to the bartender, "Please give me one beer and a double shot of vodka but put it in a plastic cup."

To which the bartender replied,
        "Don't tell me that Sister is back in here again!"

The New Contemplative Monk

The other day, a young man walked into a Monastery and said,
"I want to be Monk."

Wanting to make sure the guy knew what he was getting himself into, the Abbot explained to him that in their Monastery, "Silence was the Golden Rule."

The brothers are allowed only say two words per year.
And, those words could only be told to the Abbot.

"I think that I'll love it," said the man.

After his first year in the Monastery,
the young man goes was called to the Abbot's Office.

"Well, my son," the Abbot said, "what do you have say?"

The man replied, "Bed's Hard."

"I'll see what I can do to help you get a softer bed.
Be blessed, my child!" said the Abbot.

At the end of the young man's second year in the Monastery,
the young man is once again summoned into the Abbot's Office.

"Well, my son," the Abbot said, "what do you have say?"

"Food Bad!" the young man said.

"I'm sorry to hear that." responded the Abbot.
"I'll see what I can do to help improve the quality of the food."

After the young man's third year in the Monastery,
he was once again brought into the Abbot's Office.

"Well, my son," the Abbot said, "what do you have say?"

"I Quit!!" the young man said.

To which the Abbot replied, "That figures since all you do is complain!"

What Do You Want to Be?

Sister Mary Thomas asked her class what they wanted to be when they grow up.

"I want to be a Doctor." little Michael said.

"I want to be a Nurse," little Malinda said.

"I want to be a Prostitute," little Jane said.

"What?!" sister screamed in shock. "Young lady, I'll see you after class!"

After class had ended, Sister Mary Thomas asked Jane,
"What did you say you wanted to be when you grew up?"

"Sister, I said I want to be a prostitute when I grow up." Jane answered.

After a big sigh of relief, Sister said,
"Oh, I thought you said you wanted to be a Protestant!"

The Catholic Church in Las Vegas

Did you know that are more Churches in Las Vegas than casinos?

During Sunday services at the offertory, some worshipers actually contribute casino chips instead of cash. I would guess that some are sharing their winnings while other are hoping to win.

Since the churches get chips from so many different casinos, the diocese now requires the parishes to send all the chips into the Diocesan Finance Office for sorting.

Once sorted into the respective casino chips, a Benedictine Priest takes the chips to each of the casinos and exchanges them for the cash.

Around the diocese, he is officially known as The Chip Monk.

Two Partying Priests

Late one afternoon, Father Joe went up to Father Frank and said,
"I am SICK and TIRED of always having to be the priests.
I wish that we could have just one night where we could just go out and let loose. We could go to the Casino, go to the bar and just have a good time. I just want one night when we could just 'Party Like It's 1999.'"

Father Frank was shocked. "Are you nuts?" he shouted.
"This is a small town and everyone knows us. If we go to any of the local clubs, we're all but guaranteed to run into someone we know."

Fr. Joe said, "That's alright, Frank, because I've got a plan.
We could drive over to our neighboring state and go to their casinos. Over there, we could play the slot machines, play Blackjack and Poker and even drink if we want to drink. Nobody knows us over there."

"Well Joe," said Fr. Frank, "if you think that it will work, let's give it a ry."

So, later that night Fr. Joe and Fr. Frank headed across the state border.
They had a good time going from Casino to Casino.
They played cards and drank beers seemingly forgetting that they were both priests.

After dragging themselves back into the Rectory at about 5 o'clock the morning, Fr. Fred began to feel really bad.

"Joe, Man, we should have never done that." said Fr. Frank.
"As we priests should never be hanging out in Casinos, gambling and drinking. It's just not right! Even if the people never find out what we've done, God will always know."

"I understand how you feel," said Fr. Joe, "and I've got a plan.
"Tomorrow morning, we'll get up and go into the church.
You can hear my confession and I can hear your confession.
That way, we can make this right with God."

"That's a great idea." said Fr. Frank.

Early the next morning, Fr. Frank put on his vestments and haded into the confessional. Not long after, Fr. Joe came in, knelt down and said,

> "Bless me, Father, for I have sinned. Last night, my priest friend and I went over to the Casinos. We gambled, got drunk and dragged ourselves into the rectory at about 5 o'clock in the morning. I really do feel bad. I hope that God and you will forgive me."

Fr. Frank answered, "The Lord is patient and forgiving, and so shall I be.
> For you penance, why don't you say 5 Hail Mary's,
> 5 Our Father's and donate 10 dollars to the poor
> and you will be absolved of your sin."

"Thank you," said Fr. Joe.

After a short while, they switch sides and Fr. Frank began his confession.
> "Bless me, Father, for I have sinned." he said.
> "Last night, my priest friend and I went over to the Casinos.
> We gambled, got drunk and dragged ourselves into the rectory
> at about 5 o'clock in the morning. I also do feel bad.
> I hope that God and you will forgive me."

After a short pause, Fr. Joe shouted, "I don't believe this!
> How DARE you call yourself a priest!

> If you even want to be forgiven, you will do 500 "Our Father's",
> 500 "Hail Mary's", you will donate all your money for the next month
> to the church, and go around the church 500 times on your knees praying
> for the Lord's forgiveness. Then come back and we'll discuss absolution,
> but I not promising you anything!"

"WHAT??!!" Father Frank was shocked. "What's wrong with you Joe?"

"Hey," Fr. Joe replied,
> "What I do with my free time is one thing, but I take my job seriously!"

Evaluating the New Priest

Not long after his arrival in his new assignment, Fr. Daniel was summoned to an evaluation meeting with his Pastor, Fr. Tony.

"You know," Father Tony said,
      "when you came into our parish with all your new ideas,
      I had questions about how you were going to fit in.
      I wondered how well your ideas were going to work.

When you wanted to put bucket seats down in the front two rows of seats,
      I had my doubts. But now, at every Mass, the seats are filled up with
      young people. So, I have to agree that it was a good idea.

Then, when you wanted to "jazz" up the choir and we started singing newer,
      peppier songs, I was afraid it would offend the older parishioners.
      But, now, we have a lot of new, younger choir members,
      and the music seems to pick up the services a lot more than
      the old music. So, once again I have to agree that you were right!

But when you wanted to put in the drive-through confessional,
      I have to admit I thought you'd lost it. But now, at least,
      there are more people coming to confession than ever.
      I think you've come up with another good idea.

However, I do have to put my foot down on one thing,
      the neon sign out front that says
      'Toot 'N Tell or Go to Hell' has to go!!!"

He's Going to Heaven

The other day, Father George walked into Johnny's Bar and Grill
and asked the first man he saw, "Do you want to go to Heaven?"

"I do Father," the man replied.

"Then stand over there against the wall," the priest ordered.

Father George then asked a second man, "Do you want to go to Heaven?"

"I sure do!" the man said.

"Then stand over there against the wall," said the priest.

Then Father George walked up to Johnny and asked him, "Do you want to go to Heaven?"

But Johnny said, "No, I don't!"

"I don't believe this!" Father George exclaimed.
"You mean to tell me that when you die you don't want to go to Heaven?"

"Oh," Johnny said, "when I die, yes.
But, I thought you were getting a group together to go right now."

The Pastor is Dying

An old Pastor realized that he was dying. So, he sent a message for his banker and his lawyer, both loyal parishioners, to come to his rectory.

When they arrived, they were ushered up to his bedroom.

As they entered the room, the Pastor held out his hands and motioned for them to sit on each side of the bed. The old Priest grasped their hands, sighed contentedly, smiled, and stared at the ceiling. For a time, no one said anything.

Both the banker and lawyer were touched and flattered that their Pastor would ask them to be with him during his final moments.

They were also confused; the Pastor had never given them any indication that he particularly liked either of them. They both remembered his many long, uncomfortable sermons about greed, covetousness, and avaricious behavior that made them squirm in their seats.

Finally, the banker said, "Father, why did you ask us to come?"

The old Priest mustered up his strength and then said weakly, "Jesus died between two thieves, and that's how I want to go."

School Restoration

Last week, Father Tony was talking to his Parishioners
        about the plans to restore the school building.

"This morning," he said, "I have some good news and some bad news."

"The Good new is,
        we have enough money to finally restore our school building."

"The Bad News is,
        it's still in you pockets!"

Celibacy

In an ancient monastery, a new Monk arrived to dedicate his life to the Lord. He was overjoyed when the Abbot asked him to join the other Monks as they copied many of the ancient records.

The first thing he noticed was that the Monks were copying by hand, books that had already been copied by hand. He worried that somehow mistakes could have been made on the older copies and that the Monks could have been simply copying someone else's mistakes whenever they made new copies of the ancient records.

He felt that he had to speak up. "Forgive me, Father Gregory, but copying other copies by hand might allow many chances for error. How do we know we aren't copying someone else's mistakes? Will we ever have the chance to check our copies against the originals?"

Father Gregory was startled! No one had ever suggested that before. "Well my son, that is a good point. I will take one of these latest books down to the vault and study it against its original documents."

So, Father Gregory went deep into the restricted vault. Only he was allowed inside. There he began to study the records. As it was getting late in the evening, one of the Monks realized that Father Gregory had not yet returned from the vault.

All of the brothers were getting worried about him. Finally one Monk decided to go down to the vault check on Father Gregory.

As grew closer to the door of the vault, he heard sobbing. "Father Gregory?" He called. But, the only response he received back was even heaver sobbing.

"Father Gregory, are you alright?" he called out as he continued his search.

He finally found the old Priest sitting at a table with both the new copy and the original ancient book in front of him. It was obvious that Father Gregory had been crying for a long time. "Oh, my Lord, what is wrong?" asked the Monk.

"Celebrate!" Father Gregory replied. "The word is "CELEBRATE!"

And together, they cried some more!

A Priest and a Bus Driver

The other day, a priest and a bus driver both died and went to Heaven.
When they arrived at the Pearly Gates, they were greeted by St. Peter.

St. Peter told the priest that God had a very special place picked out for him.
It was a place that God knew the priest would enjoy.

So, St. Peter took the priest on a short journey through the rolling hills of
Heaven. There in the middle of a valley they arrived at a quaint little cottage.
It was surrounded by the beauty of creation.

"Father, this will be your home for all of eternity." St. Peter told him.
"It is a perfect little cottage, right next to a lovely brook.
It has a lush little garden and a library full of books."

"Thank you so much," replied the priest. "I know that I will enjoy it here!"

Returning to the Pearly Gates,
St. Peter then takes the Bus Driver to his special place.

They journeyed through the rolling hills, past by the priest's little cottage
and headed to a large mansion. It was a huge 200-room castle that sat on one of
the mountains. It was surrounded by lake and streams, fields and valleys.

"This will be yours for eternity." St. Peter said to the Bus Driver.
"You will have servants to wait on you hand and foot,
and you can have everything you want."

Looking at the size of his new home, the Bus Driver said to St. Peter,
"Please don't get me wrong. I am grateful for this beautiful castle.
But why am I getting a house that is so much better than
that of the priest?"

St. Peter just laughed and said,
"My son, it is because you brought more souls to Heaven!

When the priest preached, everyone fell asleep.

But, when you drove your bus, everybody prayed!"

Nuns are Married to God

After suffering a serious heart attack,
    John needed to have a heart bypass surgery.

As he awakened from the surgery,
    he found himself in the care of Nuns at a Catholic Hospital.

While recovering, one of the sisters asked him questions regarding
    how he was going to pay for his treatment.

First, she asked if he had health insurance.

"No," he replied.

Then, she asked if he had money in the bank.

"Sorry, I don't have any money in the bank either." he said.

"Well, do you have a relative who could help you?" she asked.

He said, "I only have a spinster sister, who is a Nun."

Sister became agitated and announced loudly,
    "Nuns are not spinsters! Nuns are married to God."

To which the man replied,
    "Then send the bill to my Brother-in-Law."

Mother Superior and the Great Milk

As their 98 year-old Mother Superior of their community was dying,
    the Sisters in the Convent gathered around her bed
    trying to make her last journey comfortable.

She hadn't eaten anything in days and the Sisters grew worried.

Hoping to at least get her to drink something, one of the Sisters brought her some warm milk. But, the Mother Superior refused to drink it.

Trying again, they still were turned down by their dying leader.

Then one of the Sisters took the glass back to the kitchen.
Remembering a bottle of whiskey that they received as a Christmas gift,
she opened the bottle and poured a generous amount into the warm milk.

Back at Mother Superior's bed, she held the glass to her lips.

"Please drink some," she said.

Well, Mother first drank a little, then a little more and a little more.

Before they knew it, she had drunk the whole glass down to the last drop.

"Mother," the nuns solemnly asked, "Will you please give us some wisdom before you die?"

So, the Mother Superior sat up in bed and with a piously said, "Don't sell that cow."

Father Bob's Best Day of Golf

It was no secret to the world that Father Bob was addicted to golf. If he could, he would be on a golf course each and every day.

One Sunday morning, he decided that he didn't want to do the 10 A.M. Mass, so he told his colleague, a younger priest, that he wasn't feeling well. He asked the young priest to cover for him at Mass.

When the younger priest agreed, Father Bob placed a DO NOT DISTURB sign on the door to his room, threw his golf clubs in his car, and headed off for a course a few miles away.

Meanwhile, the younger priest explained to the parish that the older priest was feeling ill and could not celebrate Mass with them. He asked that the congregation pray for poor Father Bob.

Up in Heaven, St. Peter and Jesus were watching what was happening.

St. Peter turned to Jesus and asked,
        "Lord, are you going to let him get away with this?"

Jesus responded, "No....I'll take care of it."

When Father Bob arrived at the golf course and teed up on the first hole; wham....to his amazement hit a HOLE-IN-ONE.

He proceeded to the second tee, and again he hit another HOLE-IN-ONE.

Father Bob was ecstatic. He couldn't believe how well he was playing.
        As he continued to play, every hole was a HOLE-IN-ONE.

By the end of the day, Eighteen holes later, his score was an amazing 18.
        That's perfection in the golf world.

Finally St. Peter couldn't take any more.

He said to Jesus, "I thought you were going to punish this guy,
instead, he plays the round of his life....What kind of punishment is that?"

Jesus looked at St. Peter and said, "Who's he going to tell?"

Keeping Everybody Happy

The following is a summary of comments made about the parish priest:

If his homily is longer than usual:	"He sends us to sleep."
If his homily is short:	"He hasn't bothered."
If he raises his voice:	"He is shouting."
If he speaks normally:	"You can't hear a thing."
If he is away:	"He's always on the road."
If he is at home:	"He's a stick-in-the mud."
If he is out visiting:	"He's never home."
If he is in the rectory:	"He never visits his people."
If he talks finances:	"He's too fixed on money."
If he doesn't talk finances:	"The parish is dead."
If he takes his time with people:	"He wears everybody out."
If he is too brief with people:	"He never listens."
If he starts Mass on time:	"His watch must be fast."
If he starts a minute late:	"He holds everybody up."
If he is young:	"He lacks experience."
If he is old:	"He ought to retire."

And, if he dies...
Well, of course: "No one could ever do without him."

SECTION SEVEN
Family Jokes

"Sirs, what must I do to be saved?"

And they said, "Believe in the Lord Jesus and you and your household will be saved."

So they spoke the Word of the Lord to him and to everyone in his house....then he and all his family were baptized at once.

Act 16:30-33

Two Little Old Ladies

Two senior ladies met for the first time
      since graduating from high school.

One asked the other,
      "You were always so organized in school,
           did you manage to live a well planned life?"

"Oh yes," replied her friend.

      "That's why I've been married four times!"

"Four times?
      Why four times?" asked her friend.

Well, my first marriage was to a millionaire;
      my second marriage was to an actor;
      my third marriage was to a preacher;
and now I'm married to an undertaker."

Her friend asked,
      "What do those marriages have to do with a well planned life?"

To which she replied,
"One for the money,
         two for the show,
            three to get ready,
              and four to go."

Satan's Sister

Not too long ago, a young priest was standing before his congregation and
    preaching in depth about the degrees of sin in their community.

He preached about fornication.
    He preached about abominations.
        He even preached about confrontations.

He was going on and on and on about the numerous sins that were being
committed by the very same folks who looked so pious on Sunday mornings.

Well, right in the middle of his preaching,
    would you believe that Satan, himself, showed up on the Altar.

Satan looked at the Church and let out a great big roar!
    "AAAHHHHHHHHH!!!" he screamed.
    And half of the church's members ran out of the back door.

""AAAHHHHHHHHH!!!" he screamed, again.
And the other half of the church's members ran out of the back door,
    except for one older man seated in the front row.

So, Satan looked at that man and yelled, ""AAAHHHHHHHHH!!!"
    But, the man just looked at him.

So he yelled again, ""AAAHHHHHHHHH!!!"
    And, the man just looked at him.

So, Satan jumped down off of the Altar ran up the man and yelled a third time,
    ""AAAHHHHHHHHH!!!"
    But, the man just looked at him.

Well, being confused, Satan looked at the man and said,
    "Don't you know who I am? It's me, Lucifer.
    You know, the Lord of Darkness. The Prince of Evil.
    Why aren't you scared of me?

To which the man replied, "Why should I be scared of you?"

    "I've been married to your sister for 27 years."

Momma, Please Help Me!!!

Please excuse the rough language in the following story.
I would have deleted them, but the story wouldn't be the same.

After enjoying a wonderful celebration of the Sacrament of Matrimony,
a young couple headed out for their honeymoon.

The Bride truly loved her husband.
She wanted to spend the rest of her life with this wonderful man.

After returning from the honeymoon, the bride immediately called her mother.

"Well," said her mother, "so how was the honeymoon?"

"Oh, Momma," the new bride replied,
"the honeymoon was wonderful! So romantic!"

Suddenly, the bride began to cry.
"But, Momma," she sobbed, "as soon as we returned,
John started using these terrible and disgusting words.
He said words that I have never ever heard!
He was using all kinds of four-lettered words!
Momma, please help me! I have to get out of here!" She cried.

"Jill," responded her mother. "You have to calm down. You are married now
and I can't just come get you because he was using four-lettered words!
Anyway, what could he possibly be saying that would be that bad?

"I just can't tell you!" cried the new bride,
"The words are just too horrible for me to say to my Mother!"

I'm too embarrassed, they're just too awful! COME GET ME, PLEASE!!

'Baby Girl," her mother replied, "Just tell me, I can handle almost anything."
"Tell Momma those horrible four-lettered words that he said to you!"

Sobbing, the bride said, "Oh, Momma, he was using words like;
dust, wash, iron, and cook."

"I'll pick you up in twenty minutes," said the mother.

Fulfilling Their Requests

The other day, three men died
    and found themselves standing before the Judgement Seat.

Before God would allow them to enter Heaven, He gave them each a chance
    to come back to earth as anything they wanted.

The first guy said, "Lord, I want to come back as myself,
    but could you make me 100 times smarter than I am now?

    So God made him 100 times smarter.

The second guy said, "Lord, I want to be better than that guy.
    So, could you make me 1000 times smarter than he is?

    So God made him 1000 times smarter.

The last guy decided that he wanted to be the best.
    So he said, "Lord, could you make me better than both of them?
    Would you make me 1,000,000 times smarter than those two guys?"

So God made him a woman!!!

Shotgun Marriage

Early one morning, Mary awoke to find that her husband was not in bed.

So, she put on her robe and slippers and hurried down the stairs to find him.

From the bottom of the stairs, she could see him sitting at the kitchen table
    with a piece of toast and a cup of coffee in front of him.

Right away, she could tell that he was deep in thought.
    He seemed to be just staring out of the window.

Not wanting to disturb him, she watched from the stairs as he sipped his coffee
and appeared to be wiping tears from his eyes.

"Honey, " she said, "What's wrong?
                    What made you get up so early?"

Looking up from his coffee, the husband turned to her and asked,
"Do you remember 20 years ago when we were dating, and you were only 16?"

"Yes, I remember,"she replied.

After a short pause, he continued to ask,
"Do you remember when your father caught us in the back seat of my car?"

"Yes, Dear, I remember,"
    said the wife as she lowered herself into a chair beside him.

After a long sigh, the husband continued,
        "Do you remember when he shoved the shotgun in my face and said,
            either you marry my daughter,
            or I'll send you to jail for 20 years?"

"Oh yeah, I definitely remember that," she softly replied.

As he wiped another tear from his cheek, he looked up and said,
    "I would have gotten out, today."

All Hen Pecked Husbands Go to Heaven

One thing for certain is the fact that all good husbands will indeed go to Heaven.

In fact, right out side of Heaven, husbands will notice two special gates that are designed just for them.

Over one Gate hangs a sign that reads, "For Hen Pecked Husbands".

Hanging over the other Gate was a sign that simply reads, "For Husbands".

As you could guess, the line for Hen Pecked Husbands was indeed a very long line. It was filled with all of the men who were nagged, probed and prodded by their wives. The line stretched almost to the end of the clouds.

In the other line, there was only one man standing there!

St. Peter walked up to the man who was standing alone in the "For Husbands" line and curiously asked, "So, were you not nagged while you were married? Why are you in this line?"

To which the man replied,
"I don't know.... My wife told me to stand here!"

Honey, My Love

An elderly priest was invited to an old friend's home for dinner one evening.

He was impressed by the way his buddy preceded every request to his wife
    with endearing terms such as
    Honey, My Love, Darling, Sweetheart, and Pumpkin.

The couple had been married almost 60 years
    and, clearly, they were still very much in love.

While the wife was in the kitchen, the priest leaned over and said to his friend,
    "I think it's wonderful that, after all these years,
    you still call your wife those loving pet names."

The old man hung his head.

"I have to tell you the truth, Father," he said,
    "Her name slipped my mind about ten years ago
    and I'm scared to death to ask her what it is!"

Old Father Joseph

The other day, Old Father Joseph, was talking to some of the younger priests.

"My young brothers," Father Joseph said,
    "When you get to be my age
    you spend a lot of time thinking about the hereafter."

"Really," replied Fr. Norman, "Why is that?"

To which Father Joseph responded,
    "Well, I often find myself going into a room
    and thinking what did I come in here after."

Love is Eternal

An 85-year-old couple, after being married for almost 60 years, died in a car crash. They had been in good health, mainly due to the wife's interest in health food and exercising.

When they reached the Pearly Gates, St. Peter took them to their mansion. It was beautifully designed with a spacious kitchen, master bath suite and a Jacuzzi.

As they looked around, the old man asked St. Peter how much all this was going to cost. "It's free," St. Peter replied. "This is Heaven."

Next, they went out in the back yard to survey the championship-style golf course that the home bordered. They would have golfing privileges every day. As an added bonus, each week the course changed to a new one representing the greatest golf courses on earth.

The old man asked, "What are the greens fees?"
St. Peter replied, "This is heaven, you play for free."

Next, they went to the club house and saw the lavish buffet lunch with
the cuisines of the world laid out.

"How much to eat?" asked the old man.
"Don't you understand yet? This is Heaven. It is free!" St. Peter replied.

"Well, where are the low fat and low cholesterol tables?" the old man asked.

St. Peter lectured, "That's the best part about being in Heaven.
Here you can eat as much as you like of whatever you like and
you'll never get fat and you'll never get sick either.
This is, after all, Heaven."

With that, the old man went into a fit of anger, throwing down his hat and stomping around the room. His wife did her best to calm him down. Once he was calm, she asked him what was wrong.

"This is all your fault," he said.

"If it weren't for all your bran muffins and stupid vitamins,
I could have been here ten years ago!"

Taking It With Him

While on his deathbed,
    an ornery old man told his wife
        that he wanted to be buried with all of his life's savings.

So, he told her, 'When I die, I want you to take all of my money
    and put it in my casket with me. I don't want to leave a penny behind!"

He even went as far as making her promise that
    she would fulfill his last wishes.

On the day of his funeral,
    everyone watched his wife as she carried a shoe box up her husband's
    coffin and placed it carefully inside his casket.

As she turned to leave one of her good friends ran up to her
    and told her that everyone thought that it was a bad idea
    for her to bury all of their money with her husband.

(No one really liked him.)

The wife explained to her friend that
    she was a devoted wife,
        a good Catholic Mother
            and a woman of her word.

Regardless of how mean he was to her,
    she had to keep her promise to him.

So, her friend asks,
    "How are you going to support yourself without any money?"

To which she replied,
    "I think that I'll be just fine. I wrote him a check."

Gold Bricks

There once was a rich man who was near death.

He was very sad because he had worked so hard for his money
but, he knew that it would be impossible to take it with him to Heaven.

So, he began to pray that he might be able to take some of his wealth with him.

After hearing his pleas, the Angel Gabriel appeared to him and said,
"Sorry, but as you know, you can't take your money with you to Heaven."

The man begged St. Gabriel to please ask the Lord if it would be at all possible
to bend the rules and allow him to bring something with him when he dies.

The rich man prayed for many days that God would grant his wish.

After a few days, St. Gabriel once again appeared to the man.
This time, Gabriel lets the man know that God had decided to allow him
to take one suitcase with him into Heaven.[8]

Filled with glee, the man found his biggest bag
and filled it with pure gold bars. He then put the bag next to his bed.

Shortly after he died, the man showed up at the Pearly Gates
and was greeted by St. Peter. Looking at the man's large suitcase,
St. Peter says, "I am sorry, sir, but our policy is that you cannot bring anything
into Heaven with you." You'll have to check it at the curb.

So, the man explained to Peter that he had permission
and asked Peter to please check it over with the Lord.

After verifying the man's story, St. Peter told him,
"You indeed were granted this special request. But, the Lord wants me to
check what you have in the bag before we let you inside."

When he opened the bag to see what the man thought was just too precious to
leave behind, St. Peter exclaimed, "What? You brought pavement?!!!"

---

[8]God must have consulted the airlines about that one carry-on
bag rule!

Lord, Grant Me One Wish

Early one morning,
      a man was walking along a California beach was deep in prayer.

All of a sudden he said out loud, "Lord, grant me one wish."

Suddenly, a cloud appeared above his head
      and he heard a voice coming down from heaven.

"My son, because you have had the faith to ask, I will grant you one wish."

The man realized that it was the voice of God.

Falling to his knees, the man asked,
      "Lord, would you build a bridge to Hawaii,
      so I can drive over anytime I want to."

To which the Lord replied, "Your request is very materialistic.
      Think of the logistics of that kind of undertaking.
      The supports required to reach the bottom of the Pacific!
      The concrete and steel it would take!

      I can do it, but it is hard for me to justify your desire for worldly things.

      Take a little more time and think of another wish,
      a wish you think would honor and glorify me."

So, the man thought about it for a long time.
      Finally he said, "Lord, I have been married and divorced four times.
      All of my wives said that I am uncaring and insensitive.
      I wish that I could understand women.
      I want to know how they feel inside,
      what they are thinking when they give me the silent treatment,
      why they cry,
      what they mean when they say "nothing"
      and how I can make a woman truly happy?"

After a few minutes God replied,
      "So, do you want two or four lanes on that bridge?"

Mistaken Identity

The other day,
a middle-aged woman suffered a heart attack and was taken to the hospital.

While on the operating table, her vital signs began to weaken and the doctors feared that they were going to lose her.

Somehow she found herself standing before the Pearly Gates.

As St. Peter checked the list of names, he realized that a mistake had taken place and that this lady was not supposed to die.

So, he brought her before God to see what could possibly be done.

Knowing that the mishap was not her fault, the Lord graciously agreed to send her back down to Earth. In fact, because the Lord was feeling so good, He actually promised her that she would live at least another 30 or 40 years.

After returning to Earth, the woman decided that if she was going to be here for another 30 to 40 years, she should go to a plastic surgeon and put in for the works.

"If I am going to be here for that many years, I really want to look younger," she said.

So, she set up to have everything that you could imagine sucked, tucked, trimmed, and pushed up. By the time she was done, she looked like a woman who was half her age. She even made sure that she had her graying hair fried, dyed and laid to the side!

Man, she was looking good!

As she walked out of the plastic surgeon's office, after the last operation was done, she was hit by an ambulance and was immediately killed.

When she arrived at the gates again, she demanded to see the Lord.
　　　Standing before the Lord, she exclaimed,
　　　"I thought you said I had another 30 to 40 years?"

To which God replied, "I'm sorry. I didn't recognize you."

SECTION EIGHT
Children Jokes

I give you praise,
Father, Lord of Heaven
and Earth,
for although you have
hidden these things
from the wise
and the learned
you have revealed
them to the childlike.

Luke 10:21

A Big Red Bike

One day, a little boy was walking with his mother through a department store.
        As they strolled along, he looked up and saw a beautiful red bike.

He said to his mother, "Momma, I really want that bike."

"Son," she said, "right now, we can't afford that bike.
        But, maybe one day you will get it."

When they returned home, the little boy immediately ran to his room, dropped
down on his knees and began to pray for the bike.

"Lord," he prayed, "I really want that bike
        and I'll give you 24 hours to get it to me!"

Well, after 24 hours, he found himself still disappointed because he had no bike.
He believed that if he really prayed hard for something, God would give it to
you. There had to have been something wrong with his prayer.

So, he ran back to his room, dropped down on his knees and prayed,
"Lord, I really NEED that bike and I'll give you 24 hours to get it to me!"

After another 24 hours, he still had no bike. Feeling a bit distraught, he wandered
around the house trying to figure out why he hadn't received the bike.

While passing through his Grandmother's room, he noticed a homemade altar on
her dresser. On her altar, she had everything that a good Catholic Grandmother
should have: a large St. Jude Candle, St. Joseph Lucky Beans, Over-sized
Rosaries, pictures of the Holy Family, and prayer cards from all her favorite
Saints. She also had a beautiful statue of the Blessed Mother.

Standing near her altar, the little boy ever so gently removed the statue of the
Mary and quietly brought it into his room.

He then laid her on his bed,
        wrapped her in a towel
                and stuffed her in a bottom drawer.

Then he looked to Heaven and said,
        "Lord, if you ever want to see your Mother again, get me my bike!"

Father Tony and the Pre-K Kids

Back in March, Father Tony was walking across the school yard,
heading into the building to meet with the principal. As he crossed the yard,
the Pre-Kindergarten kids were out on the yard playing kickball.

You should know that whenever Father Tony walked into the school yard,
everything seemed to come to a halt. This kids loved him so much that they
always stopped what they were doing, waved to him and said "Hello."

Well, as he walked into the yard, the Pre-K kids got really excited. They stopped
their game and began to wave and yell.

"Hey Father Tony!" "Hey Father Tony!"

One of the kids knew that she was supposed to say something in front of Tony,
but she couldn't remember what to say. So, she yelled out, "Hey Uncle Tony!"

Then, all of the kids ran up to him to give him those "4-year-old, unconditional
love hugs!" But as they hugged him, he noticed a little girl who simply stood in
the back of the crowd and waved. She quietly said to him, "Hey Father Tony."

Although it was a little confusing to him, Father Tony simply waved back and
said, "Hello."

After he completed his meeting with the principal, he headed back through the
school yard on way to the rectory. As he stepped into the yard, the entire scene
repeated itself.

"Hey Father Tony!" "Hey Father Tony!" "Hey Uncle Tony!"

The kids all ran over, again, and gave him those hugs.

But, the same little girl stood at the back of the crowd and only said, "Hey Father
Tony."

Being curious, Father Tony approached the little girl, knelt down and said to her,
"Now baby, you are usually one of the first to run up, hug me and say 'Hello'.
Why didn't you hug me today?"

"Because I gave you up for Lent!" she said.

One For You, and One For Me

Everyone always admired the large Pecan Tree in the parish cemetery. It was a beautiful tree that always seemed to be producing the biggest and best tasting Pecans. One day, two young boys filled up a bucketful of Pecans, sat down behind the tree and began dividing the nuts.

"One for you, one for me. One for you, one for me," said one boy.

His bucket was so full of Pecans, several rolled out towards the fence.

Riding his bike down the street by the cemetery was a third boy. As he passed the fence, he thought he heard voices coming from inside the cemetery.

So, he slowed down to investigate.

Sure enough, he heard a voice say, "One for you, one for me. One for you."

He immediately knew what it was. "Oh my goodness!" he thought, "It must be Satan and St. Peter dividing the souls at the cemetery!"

As he road his bike down the street, he found an old man with a cane, hobbling along. "Mister, please come quickly!" he said. "You won't believe what I heard. Satan and St. Peter are down at the cemetery dividing the souls."

The old man said, "Boy, are you crazy? I'm not coming over there. Can't you see that I'm struggling to walk as it is!"

After some hard begging from the boy, the old man hobbled over to the cemetery and heard a voice saying, "One for you, one for me. One for you, one...."

The old man whispered, "Boy, you ain't lying. Let's see if we can see what the Devil looks like." Shivering with fear, they crept toward the cemetery fence, but they were unable to see anything.

Suddenly, they heard a voice say, "One for you, one for me. One for you, one for me. And one last one for you. That's all!.... Now, let's go get those nuts by the fence, and we'll be done."

They say the old guy made it down the street 10 minutes before the boy could!

The Collar

The other day, Father Mike was walking to the school when a group of young students came running towards him. After stopping to greet each of them, Father Mike asked them if they had any questions for him.

Little Johnny, the youngest one in the group, raised his hand and asked,
> "Why do you priests dress so funny?
> You look like you have your shirt on backwards."

Father Mike explained to the kids that his Roman Collar was a part of his uniform and that all priests were supposed to wear their uniform when they were doing priestly stuff.

Just like students wear school uniforms, priests wear uniforms that let everyone know that they are priests.

"But, why does it look so funny? And, what's that silly thing on your neck?" Johnny asked.

Becoming a little perturbed by the boy's senseless questioning, tried to flip the script. So, he tarted to ask Johnny some questions.

"How old are you?" the priest asked.

"I'm 5." Johnny said.

"Do you know how to read?" the priest asked.

"Yes, do know how to read!" Johnny snapped back.

The priest took off his collar and handed it to Johnny. On the back of the collar's white tab were raised letters that list the name of the manufacturer.

"Well, Mr. Smarty-Pants," the priest said, "tell me what these letters say."

Looking intently at the letters Johnny said,
> "Kills ticks and fleas for up to six months!"

The Doorbell

The other day, Father Derran was walking down the street when he noticed a
very small boy trying to ring the doorbell on a house.

The boy was very short and the doorbell was too high for him to reach.

After watching the boy's struggles for a short time,
    Father Derran moved closer to the boy.

He crossed the street, walked up behind the little guy,
    placed his hand kindheartedly on the child's shoulder,
    leaned over and gave the doorbell a solid ring.

Crouching down to the child's level,
    the priest smiled benevolently and asked,
    "And now what, my little man?"

To which the boy replied, "Now we run!"

Gray Hair

One day, a little girl was sitting in the kitchen
    and watching her mother wash the dishes at the sink.

When she noticed that her mother had several strands of white hair sticking out
from her beautiful black hair, she looked at her mother and curiously asked,
"Momma, why are some of your hairs turning white?"

Her mother replied, "Well, every time that you do something wrong and make
me cry or unhappy, one of my hairs turns white."

After thinking about this great revelation, the little girl replied,
    "Is that why ALL of Grandma's hairs are white?"

Why Does a Bride Wear White?

Susan was attending a wedding for the very first time.
>She loved all of the flowers, the music and the happy people.
>And, she really loved the beautiful Bride's wedding gown.

In the middle of the service, she leaned over to her mother and asked,
>"Mommy, why is the bride dressed in white?"

Her mother replied,
>"She wearing white because white is the color of happiness,
>and today is the happiest day of her life.'"

Susan thought about this for a moment and then asked,
>"So why is the groom wearing black?"

Please Don't Let Me Be Late

Little Diane was dressed in her Sunday best and was running as fast as
>she could, hoping that she would not be late for Sunday School.

As she ran, she prayed, "Dear Lord, please don't let me be late!
>Dear Lord, please don't let me be late!'"

While she was running and praying, she tripped on a curb and fell. All of her
clothes got dirty and she ripped the bottom of her dress.

But, she got up, brushed herself off, and started running again!

As she ran, she once again began to pray,
>"Dear Lord, please don't let me be late....
>But please don't push me either!"

God is Watching the Apples

As the First Grade students of Our Lady of Lourdes Catholic School lined up for lunch in the cafeteria, they noticed a table that was covered with apples.

Loudly and clearly they heard Sr. Mary Edmund announcing to the group, "Make sure that you take only one apple! Remember God is watching!"

As they moved passed the apples, they also noticed a table that held a platter of chocolate chip cookies. As they got close to the cookies, little Johnny turned to his friend and said, "Hey, take all the cookies you want. God is watching the apples!"

The Lord is Out There

One afternoon a little boy was playing outdoors. He used his mother's broom as a horse and had a wonderful time until it was getting dark.

As he ran inside, he left the broom on the back porch.

As his mother was cleaning up the kitchen, she realized that her broom was missing. So, she asked her young son if he knew where the broom could be.

"It's on the back porch." he told her.

She then asked him if he would please go get it.

"Momma, you know that I'm afraid of the dark.
        Please don't make me go out there." he begged.

His mother smiled and said, "Don't worry. The Lord is out there, too."

So, the little boy opened the back door and yelled,
        "Lord, if you're out there, would you please hand me the broom?"

Sick in Church

A little girl was in church with her mother when she started feeling ill.

"Momma," she said, "can we leave now?"
    "No," her mother replied.

"Well, I think I'm going to throw up!" the little girl said.

"Then go out the front door and around to the back of the church and throw up behind the bushes!" her mother said.

After about 60 seconds, the little girl returned to her seat.

Did you throw up?" the Momma asked.
    "Yes, I did!" replied the little girl.

"How could you have gone all the way to the back of the church
        and come back so fast?" the Momma asked.

"I didn't have to go out of the church, Momma. They have a box next to the front door that says, 'For the Sick'."

Come in or Stay Out!

Like most little boys, Johnny was a professional at getting into trouble
        and trying to weasel his way out of it.

He always came up with the best excuses as to why he shouldn't be in trouble.

Tired of his stories, his exasperated mother, said to him,
        "Son, how do you expect to get into Heaven?"

Little Johnny thought it over and said,
        "Well, I'll just run in and out and in and out
        and keep slamming the door until St. Peter says,
        'For Heaven's sake, Johnny, either come in or stay out!'"

Helping the Preacher

After Father Tony had finished one of his long sermons,
>he headed to the back of the Church to greet the people.

Standing on the steps of the church,
>he shook the hands of all the men and kissed all of the ladies.

After shaking the a few of the youths' hands,
>the young son of Deacon Brian approached him.

"Good morning, little Brian," Father Tony said
>as he reached down to shake the young man's hand.

But instead of reaching up the shake the priest's hand,
>little Brian reached up and put something Father Tony's hand.

"What's this?" Father Tony asked.

"It's money," Brian said, "and it's for you!"

"Thank you, Brian," replied the priest,
>"but I don't want to take you money."

"Please take it, Father." insisted the boy.
>"My daddy says you're the poorest preacher we ever had
>and I want to help you."

Goat for Dinner

A young couple invited their elderly priest for Sunday dinner with their family. While they were in the kitchen preparing the meal, the priest asked their son what they were having for dinner.

"Goat," the little boy replied.
"Goat?" replied the startled man of the cloth, "Are you sure about that?"

"Yep," said the little boy, "I heard my Daddy say to Momma,
>'Today is just as good as any to have the old goat for dinner.'"

To Be Like Jesus

One day, Denzel walked into the family room and asked his Father,
"Dad, when will I get my own car? I really want a Jeep!"

His Father told him,
"I don't know when you'll get a Jeep.

First, your hair is too long.
Second, your grades are too low.
And third, you haven't been going to Mass on a regular basis.

So, until I see some changes in your behavior,
you can stop hoping to get your own vehicle."

A little perturbed, Denzel decided that he would try to show his Father that he was a changing man. So, he picked-up the Family Bible and headed to his room.

A few hours later, he returned to the Family Room
to discuss with his Father all that he had read.

"Dad," he said, "I've been reading the Bible and I have decided that want to be just like Jesus! I am hoping that if I can be like Jesus, you will finally get me my Jeep!"

His Father was elated to hear his son's new revelation.
And he promised that if his son would be like Jesus,
he would indeed get a new car.

"Good," Denzel replied, "because I read in the Good Book, that
Jesus had long hair,
He hung out with His friends
and they often had wine to drink!

So, I want to be just like Him!
If it was good enough for Jesus, then it's good enough for me!"

To which his Father quickly responded,
"And Jesus also walked everywhere He went!"

'So Son, you be like Jesus!"

Why Some Parents Lose Their Minds

A father passing by his son's bedroom was shocked to see that his son's bed was nicely made and everything was picked up. Then he saw an envelope propped up prominently on the pillow that was simply addressed "Dear Dad".

With the worst premonition, his hands trembled as he opened the envelope and read the letter.

Dear Dad,

It is with great regret and sorrow that I'm writing you. I had to elope with my new girlfriend because I wanted to avoid a scene with Mom and you.

I have been finding real passion with Stacy and she is so nice.
But I knew you would not approve of her because of all her piercing, tattoos, tight motorcycle clothes and the fact that she is much older than I am.

But it's not only the passion. Dad, she's pregnant.

Stacy said that we will be very happy. She owns a trailer in the woods and has a stack of firewood for the whole winter.

We share a dream of having many more children.

Stacy has opened my eyes to the fact that marijuana doesn't really hurt anyone. We'll be growing it for ourselves and trading it with the other people that live nearby for cocaine and ecstasy. In the meantime, we will pray that science will find a cure for AIDS, so Stacy can get better. She deserves it.

Don't worry Dad. I'm 15 and I know how to take care of myself. Someday I'm sure that we will be back to visit so that you can get to know your grandchildren.

Love, your son John

PS: Dad, none of the above is true. I'm over at Tommy's house. I just wanted to remind you that there are worse things in life than a report card. That's in my center desk drawer.

I love you. Call me when it's safe to come home.

A Teenager's List
of Christian Pick-up Lines

1. Nice Bible.
2. You know Jesus? Me too.
3. God told me to come and talk to you.
4. I know it's not time for the "Our Father" but can I still hold your hand?
5. How about a hug, sister?
6. Do you need help carrying your Bible? It looks heavy.
7. Did it hurt when you fell from Heaven?
8. What are you plans for tonight? Feel like a Bible Study?
9. The Word says, "Give drink to the thirsty and feed the hungry." So how's about dinner?
10. You want to come over and watch "The Ten Commandments"?
11. Girl, you ought to go to Confession, 'cause you just stole my heart.
12. Would you happen to know a Christian woman that I could love with all my heart and wait on hand and foot?
13. Nice Bracelet. Is it "What Would Jesus Do?or Who Would Jesus Date?"
14. Do you believe in Divine Intervention?
15. Have you ever tried praying over dinner and a movie?
16. You know, they say that you've never really dated until you date a Catholic?
17. Excuse me, I believe one of your ribs belongs to me.
18. What do you think St. Paul meant when he said, "Greet everyone with a holy kiss"?
19. My friend told me to come and meet you, He said that you are a really nice person. I think you know him. Jesus, yeah that's His name.
20. God was just showing off when He made you.
21. When I saw you, I knew the true meaning of "rejoice and be glad."
22. I didn't know angels flew this low.
23. If God made anything more pretty, I'm sure he'd keep it for himself.
24. What's your name and number so I can add you to my "prayer" list?

Painted by God

After a pretty rough week in elementary school, Little Johnny was happy that he was spending the weekend with his Grandma. She always knew how to make him feel good.

As a treat, his Grandma decided to take him to the park on Saturday morning.

It was a beautiful day. The sky was clear, the air was crisp and the gray moss was hanging beautifully on the majestic Oak Trees.

"Johnny," his Grandma said,
"Doesn't this look like an artist created this beautiful scene?
You know, God loves you so much that He actually painted this just for you!"

"Yeah," replied Johnny, "God did it with his left hand."

"His left hand?," his Grandma responded,
"What makes you say that God did this with His left hand?"

"Because in Church we say that Jesus sits on God's right hand!" he replied.

Palm Sunday

It was Palm Sunday but because of a sore throat,
Little Johnny stayed home from Church with his Grandma.

When the family returned home, they were carrying several palm branches.

Johnny inquired as to what the branches were for.

"People held them over Jesus' head as he walked by," his brother responded.

"Wouldn't you just know it?" Johnny complained,
"the one Sunday I don't go and Jesus shows up."

SECTION NINE
Animal Jokes

God made all kinds of
wild animals,
all kinds of cattle,
and all kinds of
creeping things
of the Earth.

God saw
how good it was.

Genesis 1:24-25

Jesus Is Watching You

Late one night, a burglar broke into a house that he thought was empty.

As he tiptoed through the living room, he suddenly froze in his tracks when he heard a loud voice say, "Jesus is watching you!"

As silence returned to the house, the burglar crept forward again.

"Jesus is watching you," the voice boomed, again.

The burglar stopped dead, again.

He was frightened.

Frantically, he looked all around.

In a dark corner, he spotted a bird cage and in the cage was a parrot.

So, he asked the parrot, "Was that you who said Jesus is watching me?"

"Yes,' said the parrot.

The burglar breathed a sigh of relief and asked the parrot, "What's your name?"

"Clarence," said the bird.

"That's a dumb name for a parrot," sneered the burglar.

"What idiot would name a bird, 'Clarence?"

The parrot replied, "The same idiot who named his Rottweiler 'Jesus.'"

Taking Some Penguins to the Zoo

The other day, a man named Kevin was on his job as a city bus driver.

As he drove down the street towards the city's zoo,
  he noticed a large truck that was stranded in the middle of the street.

Being the helpful Christian man that he is,
  Kevin stopped his bus and asked the truck driver if he needed any help.

The truck driver explained that inside his refrigerated truck,
  he had a shipment of penguins that needed to be taken to the zoo.

He asked Kevin if he would be willing to take the penguins to the zoo on the bus.

Initially, the bus driver refused.
  He explained that he knew nothing about transporting penguins.

The truck driver told him that he would give him $100
  if he would be willing to take the penguins to the zoo.

Right away, Kevin agreed to the deal.

So, the truck driver opened back of his truck and together,
  he and Kevin escorted all of the little penguins on to the bus.

Once they were all in their seats and their seatbelts were fastened,
  the bus driver drove towards the zoo.

About two hours later,
  the truck driver saw the bus headed back in the opposite direction.
  It was still loaded with all of the penguins.

After flagging the bus down, he yelled to the bus driver,
"Hey buddy, I thought that I gave you $100 to take these penguins to the zoo."

"You did," Kevin yelled back.
  'We had money left over. So, now we are headed to the movies!"

The Donkey Sale

A priest was trying to sell a donkey. With the economic recession and depression, it is really hard to sell donkeys in this modern age.

After waiting for a day,
 the priest finally found a young man who was willing to buy his donkey.

Once they agreed on the price, the priest said to the young man,
 "Son, before I let you leave with the donkey,
 I have to tell you that donkey had been trained in a very unique way.

 "Instead of using the usual words, like 'getty up' or 'whoa,'
 I used church words to tell the donkey when to go and when to stop.

 So, only way to make the donkey go, is to say, 'HALLELUJAH!.'
 the way to make him stop, is to say, 'AMEN!'"

The young man thought to himself, that's pretty cool.
 It won't be bad to have a religious donkey around the farm.

So, he paid the priest for the donkey
 and immediately got on the animal to try out the preacher's instructions.

"HALLELUJAH!," shouted the man and the donkey started walking.

 "AMEN!,"shouted the man and the donkey stopped.

"HALLELUJAH!," the man shouted again.
 And once again, the donkey started walking.

 "AMEN!,"he shouted and the donkey stopped.

He decided that he would really test out his new religious donkey.

So, he took his donkey to the foot of the mountain,
 climbed on its back and yelled out, "HALLELUJAH!."

The donkey started walking.

Again, he yelled, "HALLELUJAH!"

The donkey started to trott.

"HALLELUJAH!"

The donkey started to run.

Soon, the man realized that he was coming close to the edge of the cliff.

But, the problem was he had forgotten what he was supposed to say to make the donkey stop.

He remembered that it was a church word.

So, he began to yell out anything he could remember.

> 'Pew!"
> "Usher!"
> "Candle!"
>
> 'Celibacy!" (Everything stops with celibacy!)

As he drew close to the cliff's edge, the guy started to pray.

> 'Lord, I am your humble servant.
> I bought this donkey because I wanted to help the priest.
> I can't remember what I'm supposed to say.
> But, I know that you know.
> I know that you will help me!
>
> In Jesus name, I pray. Amen!"

And, the donkey stopped just at the edge of the cliff!

The young man got so excited that he yelled out, "HALLELUJAH!"

The Missionary and the Lion

The other day, a missionary priest was walking back to his village in a remote part of Africa when he noticed a very big lion sitting at the top of the hill. As the priest walked along, he prayed to the Lord for protection from the lion.

But as he prayed, he noticed that the lion was coming down the hill in his direction. "Lord," he prayed, "You know that I am you servant.
I have been doing all that I can do to bring people to you.
This week, I baptized and confirmed more than 500 hundred people.
I know that you are going to protect me from this lion."

When he finished praying, the lion pounced on him and pinned him to the ground.

"Lord," the priest prayed in protest,
"I though that you would save me.
Could you at least make this a Christian Lion?"

And immediately the Lion made the Sign of the Cross and began to pray,

"Bless us, O' Lord, and these thy gift
which we are about to receive from thy bounty through Christ, our Lord. Amen"

Running from the Bear

Once there were two friends walking through the woods.
When suddenly, a bear came up behind them.

As they walked faster, one of the friends reached into his gym bag and pull out his brand new pair of Air Jordan Tennis Shoes.

As the walk forward, he began to put on his new shoes and to tie them really tight. The other guy looked down at him and said,

"Why are you putting on those shoes? You'll never out run that bear."

And his friend looked up and said,
"I don't have to outrun that bear. I only have to out run you!"

SECTION TEN
Football Jokes

Give thanks to
the LORD
who is good,
whose love
endures forever!

Psalm 107:1

Congratulation to the New Orleans Saints - Super Bowl XLIV Champions
February 7, 2010

Pope John Paul II Visits a Saints Fan

The other day, a New Orleans Saints Fan was praying very hard in his room, when suddenly he had a vision of Pope John Paul II. Knowing that this was a once-in-a-lifetime chance to have a private conversation with our beloved Holy Father, he asked the Holy Father the two questions that have always been burning in his heart.

"Your Holiness, back in 1987, you came to New Orleans and visited the Superdome. After your visit, the New Orleans Saints finally became a winning team! So, I only have two burning questions that only you can answer. You see, I love the New Orleans Saints and I really need to know if there is a Superdome in Heaven? and Will I ever see 'Our Boys' play in the Super Bowl?"

John Paul replied saying, "Well, my Son, I don't know the answers to your questions, but I am willing to talk to God and get back to you."

The next day the man was once again praying in his room and the Holy Father once again appeared to him. This time the Pope knew the answers to the man's questions after having the chance to talk to God.

As the man looked up at the angel-like appearance of the Pope, the Holy Father said to him, "My son, I had a chance to talk to God. And, I have some good news and some bad news for you. The good news is there is indeed a Superdome in Heaven. In fact, the Heavenly Superdome is the only place where the Super Bowl is played up there. It is the HOME of the Saints! And, since your team is the New Orleans SAINTS, they play in the Heavenly Super Bowl, every year. In Heaven, the SAINTS never lose a game!

Believe it or not, God has already paid for you to have a ticket on the 50 yard line of the Heavenly Dome so that you will have the best seat in the house for the Super Bowl. Finally, after all these years, you will get to see *Your Boys* win the Super Bowl."

"Holy Father," the man replied, "That's the best news that you could have ever given me." "Our Boys, the New Orleans Saints, in the Super Bowl! My prayers have finally been answered."

"But, if that is the good news, Holy Father, just what is the bad news?"

The Pope looked up and replied, "Your ticket is for tomorrow's game!"

Boudreaux Goes to Hell

The other day, Old Boudreaux died and was on his way down to Hell.

Knowing what kind of person Boudreaux was, the Devil got so excited that he turned up the thermostat to make it extra warm for that old Cajun Rascal.

When Boudreaux arrived, the Devil asked,
>"Hey Boudreaux, how do you like it down here?"

Boudreaux said.
>"Man, it's just fine. It reminds me of summer times on the bayou."

Well you know, that made the Devil some mad. So, that night, he turned the thermostat up all the way that it could go. Man it was hot!

When Boudreaux woke up, the Devil asked him,
>"How do you like it down here, Now?"

Boudreaux says,
>"Man, it's fine. I kind of love it. It reminds me of August in Lafayette."

As you might expect, that made the Devil even more mad.

So, that night, he turned the thermostat down all the way that it could go!
>Instead of making it hot, he made it super cold.
>The whole place froze over.
>There was even Icicles hanging off the Devil's front porch.

When Boudreaux woke up, the Devil asked him,
>"How you like it NOW, BOUDREAUX?"

Well old Boudreaux, shivering, with blue lips and tears in his eye, said,
>"Old Devil, I sure am one happy Cajun."

"What do you mean you're one happy Cajun?" an angry Devil said.
>"It's freezing down here!"

To which Boudreaux, replied
>"Them Saints done won the Super Bowl!!!"

A Ticket to the Super Bowl

The other day, a football fan bought a ticket to see the New Orleans Saints play in the Super Bowl. Although he was excited that the Saints were finally playing in the NFL's Championship Game, he was a bit disappointed that his seat was at top of the stadium. It was so high that he could barely see the field.

During the 1st quarter of the game, he noticed a vacant seat down on the third row of the bottom section. It was right in the middle, on the 50-yard line!

So, he watched the seat for that whole quarter. He thought to himself, if no one sits there by the end of this quarter, I am going down to claim that seat.

When the 2nd quarter started, no one had come to claim the seat. So, he walked down from his nose-bleed seat and headed to the bottom section of the stadium. As he got close to the empty seat, he noticed an older gentleman sitting in the seat that was adjacent to the vacant one.

"Excuse me sir," he said to the older man, "is anyone sitting in that seat?"

"No, Son, come on in," the man replied. "Have a seat."

A few minutes later, the Saints fan asked the older gentleman if he knew to whom the seat belonged and why they weren't here at such an important game.

The man explained that he and his wife had been New Orleans Saints Fans since the team came to New Orleans. Each year they promised one another that if the Saints ever made it to the Super Bowl, they would buy tickets for the game.

He went on to explain that a few days ago, his poor wife passed away.

Feeling sorry for the nice man, the young man if he didn't have a child, a friend or even a family member that could have come to the game with him.

The man said, "No Son, they're all at the funeral."

Antagonizing the Nuns

Sister Angela and Sister Greta were at the New Orleans Saints football game and having a great time pulling for their favorite team.

Seated behind them were three young men who decided to mess with the two Nuns. The men were hoping to get the Nuns to move another section so that they could be free to rant and rave or fuss and cuss during the game.

> (They could only imagine what would happen to them
> if they cussed in front of the Nuns.
> They probably had flashbacks to
> bars of soap in the principal's office.)

They thought that if they could antagonize the Nuns,
> the two Sisters would decide to move.

So, one of the men said loudly to his friends,
> "I think I want to move to California.
> I heard that there are only 100 Catholics living there...."

The second guy said in reply, "Well, I want to move to Washington.
> I believe that there are only 50 Catholics living there...."

The third guy said, "I want to move to Idaho.
> I read that there are only 25 Catholics living there...."

One of the nuns turns around and sternly said to the three guys,

> "Why don't you go to Hell?
> There aren't any Catholics living there."

Applying Football Words to Church

In a very real way, football terminology can apply directly to our experiences as Church. For much of what takes place on Sundays, on the gridiron of a football field, also takes place on Sunday on the Battlefield of the Lord.

Here are some words that can be used both at a football game and in Church!

Blocking:

Football - On the field, blockers position themselves in front of the defenders in order to prevent them from getting to the Quarterback.

Church - A Church, Blocking is when you talk endlessly to the Pastor after Mass thus preventing others from getting to him!

Draft Choice:

Football - On the field, a Draft Choice is a person who has been picked to play on a specific team during the annual NFL Draft.

Church - In Church, a draft choice is what happens when that Little Old Lady in the Sweater comes in to Church and begins looking for the Air Conditioning Vents before she chooses here seat.

End Zone:

Football - On the field, the End Zone is the part of the field where touchdowns are scored.

Church - In Church, the End Zone are the particular pews where the priest's homily topics actually make sense.

Extra Point:

Football - On the Field, an Extra Point is what you get if you kick the ball between the goal posts after a touch down.

Church - At Church, an extra point is what you get when you tell the young associate that his sermon was too long.

Illegal Motion:

> Football - On the field, an Illegal Motion is when an offensive person is penalized for moving before the play is started.

> Church - In Church, Illegal Motion is when you should be penalized for leaving Church before the final blessing.

Defensive Interference:

> Football - On the field, Defensive Interference is when the defender hits the offensive wide receiver before the football arrives.

> Church - In Church, interference is when the priest begins to tell the Church about an up-coming change in the way we do things and you start shaking your head (no) before you let him finish.

Two-Minute Warning:

> Football - On the field, the Two-Minute Warning is when the referee blows his whistle and alerts both teams that there are only two minutes left in the half or in the game.

> Church - In Church, the two minute-warning is when that same little old Lady in the front row starts looking at her watch to tell the preacher that his sermon has gone too long and that she will only be awake for about two more minutes.

Quarterback Sneak:

> Football - On the field, the Quarterback Sneak is when the quarterback runs the football through the center of his blockers rather than handing it off to the running back, like everyone expects him to do.

> Church - In Church, the Quarterback Sneak is when you get communion and head straight for the exits thinking that no one (including God) sees you leaving Church early.

Who would have thought that Football terminology and church activities can go hand in hand?

I guess that it takes a really good preacher to interpret the words for us.

Safe Haven

There once was a young boy who was taken from his home because he was being physically abused. But, after being in the orphanage for a few weeks, he went to his social worker and told her that he wanted to leave. So, the social worker asked him, "Well, do you want to go back and live with your father, again?"

"No," said, the little boy. "He beats me."

So, the social worker asked, "Do you want to live with your mother?"
    To which the little boy replied, "No, she beats me too."

"Well, then," asked the social worker,
    "If you don't want to live with your father and you don't want to live with your mother, then who do you want to live with?"

And, the little boy answered, "The New Orleans Saints."

"The Saints?" responded the social worker.
    "Why do you want to live with the New Orleans Saints?"

"Because," replied the little boy, "They don't beat anybody."

Three Old Football Fans

Three old football fans were in a church, praying for their teams. The first one asks, "Oh Lord, when will the Dallas Cowboys win another Superbowl?"

God replies, "In the next five years." "But I'll be dead by then," says the man.

The second one asks,
    "Oh Lord, when will the Atlanta Falcons win the Superbowl?"

God answers, "In the next ten years." "But I'll be dead by then," says the man.

The third one asks,
    "Oh Lord, when will the *New Orleans Saints* win the Superbowl?"

And, God answers, "I'll be dead by then!"

A Rottweiler Saints Fan

A guy walked into a bar with his Rottweiler in tow. All of the bar patrons noticed that the big dog was wearing a Saints Jersey and a Helmet and it was holding a set of Black and Gold pom poms.

The bartender said, "Hey, Bud! No pets allowed in here! You'll have to leave!"

But, the man begged the bartender to allow them to stay by saying,
"Look I'm desperate. We're both big Saints fans and my TV is broken. This is the only place that we can see the game!"

Well, after securing a promise that the dog would behave and warning him that if there was any trouble they will be thrown out, the bartender relented and allowed them to stay in the bar and watch the game.

The game began with the Saints getting the kickoff, Reggie Bush catching it and running it back 95 yards for an game opening Touchdown!

When Reggie crossed the goal line, the Rottweiler jumped up on the bar and ran up and down the bar - high-fiving all of the bars patrons.

That bartender said to the man, "Wow, that's amazing!"

Well, as the game went on, every time the New Orleans Saints scored, the dog either high-fived the crowd, did somersaults on the bar or barked to the tune of *"When the Saints Go Marching In."*

After the game, the bartender said, "Wow, that dog is the most amazing thing I've ever seen! What will it do if the Saints win the Superbowl?"

"I don't know," replied the owner, "I've only had him for forty years."

John Elway Goes to Heaven

After living a full life, old John Elway passed away and moved on to glory.

When he got to Heaven, God, Himself, was showing John around the Kingdom.

Soon, they came to a modest little house with a faded Denver Broncos flag in the window. "This house is yours for eternity, John," said God. "This is very special; not everyone gets a house up here."

John felt special, indeed, and walked up to his house.

On his way up the porch, he noticed another house just around the corner.

It was a 3-story mansion with a Black and Gold sidewalk,
a 50 foot tall flagpole with an enormous New Orleans Saints logo flag,
and a Fleur-de-Lis emblem in every window.

John looked at God and said.
      "God, I'm not trying to be ungrateful, but I have a question.
      "I was an all-pro QB, I won 2 Super Bowls,
      and I even went to the Hall of Fame."

God said, "So what's your point, John?"

      "Well, why does Reggie Bush get a better house than me?," John asked.

God chuckled, and said, "John, that's not Reggie's house, it's **MINE**."

Books by Fr. Tony

don't be
stupid!

Lessons You Should Already Know

I have had some of the world's best teachers. But, of all my teachers, the greatest has always been my Momma. She taught me about life and unconditional love. My love for God, my love for my family and my love for myself flows from the love of my Momma. She is a no-nonsense, "straight from the hip" mother. Rather than complicating the concept, she just "tells it like it is." I am who I am today, because she answered the Call to be a Momma.

One of the very first lesson that I learned early in life was that *ignorance is when you don't know something.* If you don't know that it is wrong, you can plead ignorance. But, *stupidity is when you know something is wrong but you still do it!* You can't plead ignorance, you are just stupid!

This book is a collection of spiritual lessons that I have learned from all of my teachers, especially my Momma and my Lord and Savior, Jesus Christ. I pray that this collection of lessons will be a blessing to you and all you love.

Rev. R. Tony Ricard, M.Th., M.Div.
A Priest of the Archdiocese of New Orleans
and His Momma's Baby

I Still Believe!

A Testimony of Faith After the Storm!

I Still Believe!
A Testimony of Faith After the Storm!

Rev. R. Tony Ricard, M.Th., M.Div.
A Priest of the Archdiocese of New Orleans
and Hurricane Katrina Survivor!!

On August 29, 2005, life as I knew it was changed forever.

Never could I have imagined the pain and heartache that we, the **Katrina Survivors**, would have to endure.

Yet, somehow, we are surviving. Somehow, we are making it. And, somehow, **We Still Believe**!

We know that it is through God's Grace that we have been able to make it.

As I look back on my post-Katrina journey, I realize now, more than ever, how much God loves us. The reflections in this book speak about keeping the faith in tough times.

As the old folks would say,
"As long as there is a God in Heaven, I know that I am going to be alright!"
With this faith, now offered to you is My Testimony of Faith After the Storm!

Rev. R. Tony Ricard, M.Th., M.Div.
A Priest of the Archdiocese of New Orleans *and* Hurricane Katrina Survivor!

MAXimum Faith

Prayers and Reflections by Young Katrina Survivors

edited with an introduction and prayers by
Rev. R. Tony Ricard, M.Th., M.Div.
and Mr. Chris A. Quest, II

Proceeds from the distribution of the *MAXimum Faith* prayer book
and the book *I Still Believe!*
go towards providing academic scholarships,
assisting with youth ministry programs
and the continuation of the print/prayer ministries of
Two Knights Publishing Co.

For more information, please visit
www.FatherTony.com

COMING 2010

A Documentary Film by Cynthia Capen

A documentary film entitled *Father Tony* is currently in post-production in Los Angeles, California. It's an inspirational story of Father Tony Ricard, a black Creole New Orleans Catholic Priest, and Pastor of Our Lady Star of the Sea Catholic Church on St. Roch Avenue in the poor 8th Ward. For the past 5 years, independent producer Cynthia Capen and her camera crew followed and filmed the struggles and triumphs of Father Tony. The film is a collective and quite touching portrait of Father Tony's deep and abiding faith and his exuberate and often humorous style of preaching. His powerful gift for evangelical youth ministry is becoming nationally known.

In recent years, the image of the Catholic Priest has been blurred with scandals. This documentary film offers a fresh perspective on this millennial old vocation by delving into the life of a man who loves being a priest. Viewers will get an intimate glimpse of Father Tony's unshakeable faith during the most difficult test of his priesthood – the aftermath of Hurricane Katrina where he says he was transformed from a "boy" priest to a "man" priest. The documentary takes you on a journey of Father Tony's world including the culturally and historically rich City of New Orleans.

For further information contact:
Cynthia Capen – Executive Producer
Capen Communications
909.226.2941
cythiacapen@yahoo.com